# Bluegrass Gospel

T0413307

# Bluegrass Gospel

## The Music Ministry of Jerry and Tammy Sullivan

Jack Edward Bernhardt

Foreword by Bill C. Malone / Afterword by Marty Stuart

University Press of Mississippi / Jackson

The University Press of Mississippi is the scholarly publishing agency of the Mississippi Institutions of Higher Learning: Alcorn State University, Delta State University, Jackson State University, Mississippi State University, Mississippi University for Women, Mississippi Valley State University, University of Mississippi, and University of Southern Mississippi.

www.upress.state.ms.us

The University Press of Mississippi is a member of the Association of University Presses.

Material from chapter 3 was previously published in Glenn Hinson, vol. ed., *The New Encyclopedia of Southern Culture: Volume 14, Folklife* © 2009, University of North Carolina Press.

**Publisher:** University Press of Mississippi, Jackson, USA
**Authorised GPSR Safety Representative:** Easy Access System Europe
- Mustamäe tee 50, 10621 Tallinn, Estonia, *gpsr.requests@easproject.com*

Library of Congress Control Number: 2025936371

Hardback ISBN: 9781496857675

Trade paperback ISBN: 9781496857682

Epub single ISBN: 9781496857699

Epub institutional ISBN: 9781496857705

PDF single ISBN: 9781496857712

PDF institutional ISBN: 9781496857729

British Library Cataloging-in-Publication Data available

# *Bluegrass Gospel*

## The Music Ministry of
## *Jerry and Tammy Sullivan*

Jack Edward Bernhardt

Foreword by Bill C. Malone / Afterword by Marty Stuart

University Press of Mississippi / Jackson

The University Press of Mississippi is the scholarly publishing agency of the Mississippi Institutions of Higher Learning: Alcorn State University, Delta State University, Jackson State University, Mississippi State University, Mississippi University for Women, Mississippi Valley State University, University of Mississippi, and University of Southern Mississippi.

www.upress.state.ms.us

The University Press of Mississippi is a member of the Association of University Presses.

Material from chapter 3 was previously published in Glenn Hinson, vol. ed., *The New Encyclopedia of Southern Culture: Volume 14, Folklife* © 2009, University of North Carolina Press.

**Publisher:** University Press of Mississippi, Jackson, USA
**Authorised GPSR Safety Representative:** Easy Access System Europe
- Mustamäe tee 50, 10621 Tallinn, Estonia, *gpsr.requests@easproject.com*

Library of Congress Control Number: 2025936371

Hardback ISBN: 9781496857675

Trade paperback ISBN: 9781496857682

Epub single ISBN: 9781496857699

Epub institutional ISBN: 9781496857705

PDF single ISBN: 9781496857712

PDF institutional ISBN: 9781496857729

British Library Cataloging-in-Publication Data available

# Contents

# Foreword

## *Celebrating Pentecostal Music*

I've been partial to Pentecostal singers, literally, all my life, an affinity undoubtedly inspired by the songs I heard my mother singing way back in the mid- to late 1930s during my earliest years. My mother, Maude Owens Malone, told me about her conversion to Pentecostalism, sometime in 1915, when she was swept away by the preaching, prayers, and spirited songs of a band of "holiness" Christians who came through her area of East Texas, about twenty miles west of Tyler. She became locally revered in our little cotton community for her faith, her healing prayers, and for her ardent and inspired singing. It's no wonder that such uninhibited passion in her devotion and voice made a strong imprint on the formation of my musical tastes. Long before I learned how to do academic research, I became aware that music had been integrally interrelated with Pentecostalism, and a major source of its appeal, since at least 1906 when the Holy Spirit descended upon the believers at the Azusa Street Revival in Los Angeles. Like many of the early Pentecostal gatherings, Azusa was racially integrated. One of its leading preachers, in fact, was William Seymour, an African American. Mama probably knew nothing about this historic revival, considered one of the seminal events of Pentecostalism, but in her own way she contributed to the spiritual awakening that grew out of such meetings. As I grew older, I developed a skepticism about much of the theology of Pentecostalism, but I never abandoned my love for the music that came out of the movement, nor my respect for the power and conviction of its singers. Admittedly, my thinking may sometimes have been colored by romanticism, or by the tendency to see links where none existed. But I continue to believe that early religious exposure affected the singing of many American entertainers. In retrospect, it is easy for me to understand why I loved the singing of people like Molly O'Day, Wilma Lee Cooper, the early George Jones, the Bailes Brothers, Gene Watson, and Margie, Jerry, and Tammy Sullivan. Both the spirit and sound of Pentecostalism flow through their music.

When I became a scholar of country and other forms of roots-related music, I grew increasingly fascinated by the large number of musicians, black and white, who came from Pentecostal origins. Whether in the realms of gospel, rhythm and blues, soul, country, bluegrass, or rock and roll, singers emerged who could recall growing up in churches that fundamentally believed in "making a joyful noise unto the Lord." Many of these singers and musicians received their first musical training and encouragement in such environments. Accompaniment for singing might come solely from hand-clapping and a tambourine, or from a vigorously strummed guitar, but Pentecostals were also receptive to any and every kind of instrument. As soon as they could afford it, anything from a piano to an electric steel guitar to a five-string banjo or a full-fledged orchestra were granted admission to Pentecostal services. They may have sung hymns like "This World Is Not My Home," or "I Don't Want to Get Adjusted to This World," but these otherworldly-oriented worshippers nevertheless embraced any musical style that *this* world offered—whether it be ragtime, jazz, blues, or bluegrass—as long as it could be utilized to promote the word of God. My mother, in fact, remembered that the first yodeling she ever heard came in a church service somewhere there in the back country of East Texas.

While I marveled at the frequency with which Pentecostals made their marks in the shaping of American music, I nevertheless remained puzzled as to why scholars too often failed to acknowledge the phenomenon. Such interest, of course, was not entirely absent. In his 1982 essay on Elvis Presley and other rockabillies, Stephen Ray Tucker had suggested a fruitful path that academicians might follow, with his essay on "Pentecostalism and Popular Culture in the South: A Study of Four Musicians" (*Journal of Popular Culture* 16, no. 3 [winter 1982]: 68–80).

Although Tucker's article was published over forty years ago, Pentecostalism's role in the shaping of American roots music remains largely unrecognized or undervalued. In a few of my books, I have briefly speculated about the musical influence exerted by Pentecostalism, but none of these observations have ventured very deeply into the topic. Jack Bernhardt's fine discussion of Jerry and Tammy Sullivan is therefore highly welcomed. Unlike my tentative judgments, which have been based on personal, and often impressionistic, insights, Bernhardt brings a clear-eyed analysis to the task. He does not speak as an insider, but instead brings both detachment and sensitivity to his subject. His exploration is marred by neither romanticism nor parochial obsession, nor is he slumming in an exotic culture (he isn't looking for snake-handling or holy rolling). The music, both powerful and elegant, brought him to this project.

Writing as a compassionate "outsider" who sees the humanity in that music, Bernhardt has strived diligently, and successfully, to understand and describe a culture far different from his own. He of course talks about much more than the Sullivans' faith or music; his subject, above all, is working-class culture, expressed through a Pentecostal musical lens. But his account of the Sullivans' ceaseless efforts to evangelize in song, and in the smallest of churches, where love offerings often failed to even pay for their gas, evokes the spirit of the early Pentecostal missionaries who valued religious passion over worldly success. Showing the coexistence of traditional values and modern musical practices—down-home millennial religion promoted in dynamic bluegrass style—Bernhardt pays tribute to a way of life and musical culture that are unknown to most of us. What a pleasure to have been invited to welcome the publication of a work that adds a significant element to America's multidimensional religious musical heritage.

**Bill C. Malone**
AUTHOR OF COUNTRY MUSIC USA AND EMERITUS
PROFESSOR OF AMERICAN HISTORY, TULANE UNIVERSITY

# Acknowledgments

This book would not have been written without the support and inspiration of Marty Stuart, who set in motion my journey into the lives and music of the Sullivans and their faith community in the Deep South. I am indebted to Marty and to Jerry and Tammy Sullivan, who invited me aboard their bus and took me with them across the spiritual landscape of the Deep South. My appreciation to Jerry's late wife, Zelma, and their daughter Stephanie, for their hospitality and friendship. Jerry's nephew, Brother Glenn Sullivan, spoke to me at length of his family and faith, and pastoring Victory Grove Church. A special thank you to Jonathan and Jon Gideon Causey, who carry the Sullivan legacy forward, and to Jonathan's wife, Callie Bates, who stocks the bus with her Cajun delights, jambalaya and etouffee.

Heartfelt thanks to Bill C. Malone for writing the foreword and to Marty Stuart for the afterword. As the alpha and omega of this Sullivan saga, their eloquent perspectives provide additional context for the stories in the chapters in between.

Thank you to Craig Gill, director of the University Press of Mississippi for his embrace of this project, and to his executive assistant, Katie Turner, for guiding me through the labyrinth of academic publishing. Thanks, also, to Will Rigby for his copyediting expertise. Tom Rankin, Bill Malone, Nancy Cardwell Webster, and an anonymous reviewer read and commented on an early draft; I welcomed their suggestions, most of which are found throughout the book.

My sincere thanks to Richard Hurst and the staff of the Ulster American Folk Park, Omagh, County Tyrone, Northern Ireland for hosting Jerry and Tammy Sullivan at their Appalachian and Bluegrass Music Festival.

The UNC-Chapel Hill Curriculum in Folklore sponsored campus-wide concerts. Steve Weiss, librarian at UNC's Southern Folklife Collection, has archived field tapes and interviews, field notes, performances, and photographs comprising the data upon which this study is based. David Glenn supplied the map of the states and venues I visited on Sullivan tours. The staff of the Washington County, Alabama, public library offered valuable assistance in early stages of research. Thanks to Charley Pennell for his fine work on the index.

Conversations with mentors and friends from years past have contributed in ways neither they nor I could have foreseen: The late Brig. General William B. McKean, USMC, for his counsel and belief; the late professor of anthropology Morton Fried, Columbia University, for lessons in scholarship. I am grateful to Ricky Skaggs and Doyle Lawson for illuminating the brilliance of bluegrass gospel on record and on stage. Alice Gerrard and Andy Cahan introduced me to the music culture of Mount Airy, North Carolina, and Galax, Virginia. David and Trisha Messer and family, John Paul "JP" Cormier, Steve Carpenter, Mike Coupe, and Enoch and Margie Sullivan contributed significantly to the Sullivan saga. And of course, Jonathan and Jon Gideon Causey for inviting me to observe their ministry on tour in 2023. Closer to home, I am grateful to Cindy Edwards and LaNelle Davis for their encouragement and enthusiasm. Finally, my thanks to UNC-Chapel Hill, NC State University, and Elon University for hosting Jerry and Tammy for concerts and class discussions.

My interviews for other projects contributed to an understanding of music and faith in the American South: Bill Monroe, Earl Scruggs, Curly Seckler, Jimmy Martin, Doyle Lawson Charlie Louvin, Ricky Skaggs, Mac Wiseman, Charlie Waller, and Ralph Stanley.

Finally, my love and gratitude to my wife, Lisa Napp, daughter Liliana Veronica Bernhardt, and to my Yellow Labrador companion, Scout—my girls—for their enduring patience with days of seclusion while transcribing, writing, and editing a project that seemed, at times, would never end. To them, I dedicate this book.

# Bluegrass Gospel

*I will sing to the LORD all my life;*
*I will sing praise to my God as long as I live.*
PSALM 104:33

# Prologue

Seen from the third row of Ryman Auditorium's "Confederate Gallery," the sprawling stage of Nashville's iconic venue has the appearance of "high church." Rainbow hues from black klieg lights wash over the risers like sun refracting through the stained glass windows on the building's brick façade.

It's June 1, 1994, and the "choir" for tonight's "service" is a who's who of young and veteran country music stars taping a television special that will broadcast nationally on the CBS television network. The glitterati, adorned in rhinestone-festooned Nudie suits and cowboy boots, big hair, and designer gowns, are participating in *The Roots of Country: Nashville Celebrates the Ryman.*

Built between 1889 and 1892 by steamboat captain Thomas Ryman as Union Tabernacle, Ryman Auditorium was home to the Grand Ole Opry from 1943 until 1974, when country music was uprooted from downtown Nashville and remade in the image of Opryland on the outskirts of town. Produced by Quincy Jones, the television special marks reopening of the "Mother Church of Country Music" following an $8.5 million restoration project as part of revitalization for Nashville's Lower Broadway.

The program's theme song, "Brand New Church," is performed by the father-daughter gospel team of Jerry and Tammy Sullivan. The elder Sullivan composed the song with his longtime friend

3

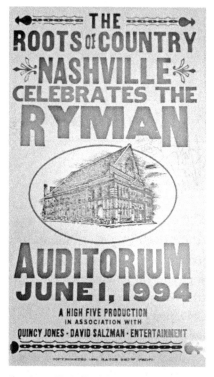

Show Poster, "Nashville Celebrates the Ryman." Hatch
Show Print, 1994.

Marty Stuart, to celebrate the symbolic rebirth of the Sullivans'
home church in Wagarville, Alabama, following a crisis of leadership. The audience, a capacity crowd of industry and media insiders
along with fans, is on its feet, clapping hands to the lively rhythm:
"Everyone's invited to our brand new church / Brand new church,
brand new church / We're all God's children, we want to share it with
you / Down at our brand new church."

The Sullivans share the stage with Stuart and Bill Monroe, the
acclaimed "Father of Bluegrass Music," the genre in which the
Sullivans render their songs of praise. After one verse, the entire
cast files on stage from the wings. Loretta Lynn, Vince Gill, Tammy
Wynette, Carl Perkins, Earl Scruggs, Kathy Mattea, Alan Jackson,

Rehearsal for *Nashville Celebrates the Ryman*. L-R: Tammy Sullivan, Bill Monroe, Marty Stuart, JP Cormier, Jerry Sullivan. Photograph by Jack Bernhardt.

Grandpa Jones and other stars of the Grand Ole Opry close the show with an ensemble chorus as the curtain falls and credits roll.

I watch the performance knowing that for the Sullivans, the night is thick with irony. Surrounded by millionaire entertainers for whom tonight is but another walk in the footlights, Jerry and Tammy seem as out of place as vegans at a pig pickin'. Not that they don't deserve to travel in such company. But the economics of this made-for-TV ensemble are a world removed from the backwoods congregations Jerry and Tammy have served since they began their musical ministry in 1979. Theirs is not the "gospel of wealth." Performing for "love offerings," pass-the-hat arrangements where audiences are asked to pay what they can afford, the Sullivans often return from touring having spent more than they earned. As the rousing chorus of "Brand New Church" is beamed to millions of viewers across the nation, the Sullivans' music and message will be heard by more people in three fleeting minutes than they have reached during their fifteen-year career.

Jerry and Tammy Sullivan may not be as well-known as their Nashville counterparts, but they are nonetheless idolized by those who know them and their music. Their 1996 CD *At the Feet of*

*God*, with gospel great Amy Grant singing harmony with Tammy, was nominated for a Grammy Award. They have appeared on The Nashville Network's *Nashville Now* with Ralph Emery and Crook and Chase shows and the *Gaither Gospel Hour*. They've performed at the Country Music Hall of Fame and in Alaska and Northern Ireland. They also played to sold-out arenas as part of the Marty Stuart–Travis Tritt "No Hats Tour" in 1992, and would return to Ryman Auditorium as featured performers in 2005.

I am in Nashville on my second tour with Jerry and Tammy Sullivan, learning and writing about their musical ministry and the faith community they serve. An anthropologist by training and journalist by accident, I have long held an interest in religion as a system of belief and its institutional orthodoxy. In 1987 I was invited to serve as country and traditional music correspondent for Raleigh, North Carolina's daily newspaper, *The News and Observer*. My responsibilities included interviewing artists and writing feature articles and concert and album reviews.

Raised Roman Catholic in northeast Ohio, I had little experience with other types of religion. As student and professor of anthropology, I had studied religion as practiced by various cultures in North and South America, Africa, Oceania, and Southeast Asia. But reading about faith and *experiencing* how faith directs behavior are different orders of learning. As music journalist and scholar, I realized I could not write insightfully about country music if I did not understand the essential role played by evangelical Protestantism in the American South.

In 1991 I received a copy of Jerry and Tammy Sullivan's *A Joyful Noise* CD, on the Country Music Foundation label and produced by Marty Stuart. I was immediately struck by their power and conviction, by Jerry's songwriting and vibrant baritone, and Tammy's elegant singing. As *The New York Times* wrote in choosing it one of its top albums of 1991, it is "Hard-picking, string-crazy Southern gospel, as ecstatic and exuberant as the best rock-and-roll."

The next year, I interviewed Marty Stuart for a story to run in advance of his concert in Raleigh. I mentioned my interest in learning about religion in the South, and that I was planning a research trip to Nashville in July. Marty invited me to phone him when I arrived, and we would explore my ideas.

Marty suggested I ride the bus with his old friends Jerry and Tammy, as he had done in the late 1980s when his music career and marriage were transitioning. Marty arranged for me to contact Jerry, who was welcoming and eager for me to join him and Tammy on their Spring 1993 tour. In April '93, I rode the bus with the Sullivans to small backwoods churches in Alabama, Mississippi, Louisiana, and Texas. My immersion in the Sullivans' ministry and music had begun.

Family groups that minister through music are immersed in a lifestyle as integral to the American South as cornbread and "Dixie." These traveling minstrels represent diverse denominations, and many perform for a broad spectrum of faith communities in venues that include churches and festivals. As practitioners of Pentecostalism, Jerry and Tammy represent a prominent subculture within the larger faith community of the American South. Such ministries have not received the scholarly attention they deserve, and Pentecostals are often stereotyped for such rare yet dramatic practices as snake handling and trance-induced hysterics.

Since the late nineteenth and early twentieth centuries, a defining feature of cultural anthropology has been the practice of fieldwork as a principal means of understanding other cultures through the interplay of experience and dialogue. Ethnographers "go into the field," living with a host community for an extended period of time, observe and participate in activities, sacred and secular, spectacular and routine. The method of participant-observation allows the ethnographer to share in people's lives as well as to observe them, opening doors to understanding the culture from the point of view of those who live it. Following the late anthropologist, Clifford Geertz, many ethnographers accept "the proposition that in understanding 'others'. . . it is useful to go among them as they go among themselves." Participant observation is one of numerous methods of data collection developed for the social sciences. But as a strategic method for anthropology it makes possible collection of many kinds of data, including oral histories and other forms of dialogue recorded in the context of their cultural setting. Through such intimate encounters with other cultural communities, ethnography's chief contributions to the social sciences include increasing awareness of cultural diversity and exploring the meaning of social life as it is held by those who act on and believe in or contest its tenets.

Over the course of fourteen years, I visited Wagarville, Alabama, where I spent time with the Sullivans in their homes, helped with chores, and traveled to and from gigs in their bus or car. Together, we attended singings at churches, festivals, university concerts and classroom lectures, and I was with them the two years they performed in Northern Ireland. I attended and recorded Wednesday, Sunday morning, and Sunday night services in their home church and recorded dozens of hours of oral histories with the family, church members, ministers, fans, and members of the community. Performances including testimonies, prayers, and acknowledgments were also recorded. I conducted archival research at the Washington County Public Library and *Washington County News*, snapped rolls of color and black-and-white photographs, and was given access to family records and heirlooms. Jerry and I, and occasionally Tammy, spoke often by phone for follow-up questions and clarification. These documents, along with my fieldnotes, comprise a rich source of data for discussion of the Sullivans' ministry, and are archived in the prestigious Southern Folklife Collection at the University of North Carolina at Chapel Hill.

Research was carried out over a period of time with repeated visits to the field. Cultures are dynamic and change. People die, others are born. Pastors and congregants may change churches. Regional demographics may change with the addition or loss of job opportunities. But the Sullivans' ministry, concerts, and faith commitment remained remarkably consistent throughout the period of my study. Jerry might make slight changes to the set list, especially in response to an audience request. His testimony would occasionally comment on current affairs, but without expressing an overt political agenda.

While Jerry and Tammy Sullivan began their ministry in 1979, they were preceded by the Sullivan Family Gospel Singers of nearby St. Stephens, Alabama. Led by Jerry's nephew Enoch and his wife, Margie Sullivan, the Family began its professional career in 1949. This book documents the lifestyle of the Jerry and Tammy Sullivan ministry on the road and at home, and the culture and environment that birthed and nurtured the Sullivans in their musical walk with God.

I write in the present tense—the "ethnographic present." This, I believe, captures the Sullivans at specific events and gives the reader a dynamic sense of the action unfolding in real time. The Sullivans, family, and friends regard their faith community as "Family in Christ," and address each other with the honorifics, Brother and Sister. While I was an outsider, the Sullivans soon began referring to me as "Brother Jack." I took this to imply their trust, and vowed to present their lives and beliefs with dignity without glossing over contradictions I might observe during the course of my research.

Many churches served by the Sullivans are located in rural, even remote, areas of the Deep South. Congregations often consist of twenty or fewer members, ages fifty and older. Some have closed their doors, and others may disappear as members die and their descendants move to cities for opportunities unavailable in the rural South. My purpose is to document the music and ministry of Jerry and Tammy Sullivan as an example of the family-based gospel music subculture that has served the South for over a century.

Jerry Sullivan died in 2014; Tammy in 2017. I was honored to deliver elegies for both friends. While these remarkable musicians have joined the Heavenly choir, their legacy continues with the music and ministry of Tammy's husband Jonathan and their son, Jon Gideon Causey. Father and son carry on the music written by Jon Gideon's grandfather and sung by his mother. The penultimate chapter follows Jonathan and Jon Gideon as they carry the Sullivans' ministry and music to the faithful, continuing a family tradition of more than seventy years.

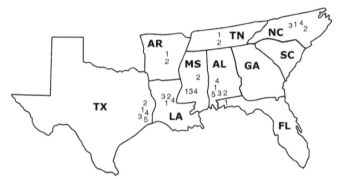

## Venues Attended by the Author on Sullivan/Causey Tours
### Location of Each Venue by State

**ALABAMA**
1 VICTORY GROVE CHURCH (WAGARVILLE)
2 PLEASANT HILL HOLINESS CHURCH (BREWTON)
3 CHURCH OF THE LORD JESUS CHRIST (GOODWAY)
4 JACKSON HIGH SCHOOL (JACKSON)
5 GOSPEL OPRY (CITRONELLE)

**MISSISSIPPI**
1 SALEM BAPTIST CHURCH (SMITH COUNTY)
2 CHURCH OF THE LORD JESUS CHRIST (PHILADELPHIA)
3 HIGH HILL BAPTIST CHURCH (SMITH COUNTY)
4 LIBERTY BAPTIST CHURCH (SMITH COUNTY)

**LOUISIANA**
1 HAPPY HOLLOW HOLINESS CHURCH (LAKE COVE)
2 LIGHTHOUSE CHAPEL OF TIOGA (TIOGA)
3 TREE OF LIFE TABERNACLE (COLFAX)
4 LONESTAR PENTECOSTAL CHURCH (BALL)

**TEXAS**
1 OAKDALE BAPTIST CHURCH (LIVINGSTON)
2 LEGGETT ASSEMBLY OF GOD (LEGGETT)
3 FIRST BAPTIST CHURCH (POINT BLANK)
4 WILDWOOD GOSPEL CHURCH (ONALASKA)
5 SHEPHERD VOLUNTEER FIRE DEPARTMENT (SHEPHERD)

**ARKANSAS**
1 LESTER FLATT MEMORIAL PARK (OTTO)
2 FIRST ASSEMBLY OF GOD (BEARDEN)

**TENNESSEE**
1 RYMAN AUDITORIUM (NASHVILLE)
2 THE PLACE OF HOPE (COLUMBIA)

**FLORIDA**
1 PINE FOREST PENTECOSTAL CHURCH (PENSACOLA)

**NORTH CAROLINA**
1 UNIVERSITY OF NORTH CAROLINA (CHAPEL HILL)
2 NORTH CAROLIINA STATE UNIVERSITY (RALEIGH)
3 ELON UNIVERSITY (ELON)
4 HOUSE CONCERT (DURHAM)

**NORTHERN IRELAND**
ULSTER-AMERICAN FOLK PARK (OMAGH)
CHURCH OF IRELAND (OMAGH)

Map by David Glenn.

In the final chapter, I reflect on what I have learned about family-based music ministries, the lifestyle, and social issues concerning faith communities as a subculture within the American South. Finally, I will share how both the ethnographer and those with whom he has traveled, lived, and learned have been changed as a result of this project.

To hear the songs referenced in the following pages, go to jackebernhardt.net.

*Chapter 1*

# Getting Acquainted

Thursday morning, April 15, 1993, my first day of fieldwork. I am met at the Mobile airport by Gerrol "Jerry" Sullivan and John Paul "JP" Cormier. Flying in from North Carolina, my image of Jerry was the black-and-white cover photo on Jerry and Tammy Sullivan's *A Joyful Noise* CD. In it, Jerry is wearing a black jacket with tie and his hair is combed up and back, well-groomed yet casual. The man introducing himself at the airport was dressed in a beige four-pocket safari shirt over faded black cotton slacks. His hair, a disheveled salt-and-pepper mane, fell in random courses over his ears and down his neck. The outer side of his black slip-on sneaker was ripped along the seam and his sock lapping over toward the floor. It wasn't the image I was expecting, but I reasoned that even gospel music stars deserve to relax.

On the fifty-five-mile drive north to Wagarville, Jerry introduces JP as an award-winning multi-instrumentalist from Nova Scotia, Canada. JP had worked as studio musician for the Canadian Broadcasting Corporation and had been voted Canada's Instrumentalist of the Year. He had worked for Enoch and Margie Sullivan and for Nashville's McCarter Sisters before joining Jerry and Tammy as a member of their band on the road and a songwriting

partner of Jerry's. JP's brother, Bob, will assist Jerry behind the wheel
of the tour bus, rolling it between the white lines from gig to gig.

JP is driving Jerry's car. Jerry asks him to play a tape of the music
they had recently recorded in Jerry's kitchen—gospel songs written
by Jerry and JP. I was immediately drawn to the quality and authenticity of the music, as hard-driving and spirited as anything I'd heard
from the national bluegrass community.

I am impressed by their enthusiasm and joy. Jerry leans over the
front seat in anticipation of a JP fiddle lick. "Listen to this coming
up," he directs us. "Here! That's beautiful, JP. Man, that's some fine
pickin'!" JP lets fly a "Whoop!," slaps the steering wheel, and rocks in
his seat each time the music reaches a crescendo of tight, pumping
rhythm. These men are absorbed by and living for their art.

We turn off US Highway 43 and pass beneath a canopy of trees
overarching the driveway to the Sullivan house. We sit at the dining
room table, sipping coffee and getting acquainted. Jerry's wife, Zelma,
a thin, soft-spoken woman is in the kitchen, washing dishes and preparing breakfast. Jerry and Zelma met in 1955 while she was working
as a waitress in a restaurant near Birmingham. They married in 1957
and have two children, Tammy, twenty-nine, and Stephanie, nineteen.

Jerry and Zelma have lived in this double-wide house trailer since
1979, and one gets the impression Zelma is the family's interior deco-
rator. Family is central to the Sullivans' lives. Photographs of Tammy
and Stephanie, Tammy's children Hanna and Trey are positioned
throughout the house, along with autographed publicity photos of
family friends Marty Stuart and Waylon Jennings, who wrote: "To
Jerry and Zelma. You deserve all of God's blessings. From Waylon."
A variety of porcelain and wooden nicknacks rest on shelves in each
room—a white wooden goose on the window sill, ceramic rooster
and hen on kitchen counter, butterfly, flower, and heart magnets
on the refrigerator door. A white macrame plant holder descends
from a ceiling beam, and ruffled curtains adorn the windows. In
the living room, chairs are furnished with wagon wheel cushions
accenting the country-themed décor. Two leather-bound Bibles sit
on bookshelves next to the back door.[1]

Jerry and Zelma in Kitchen of Wagarville home. Photograph by Jack Bernhardt.

Jerry shares with me family history, and how his nephew Emmett Sullivan had suffered a heart attack and died the week before my arrival. Jerry grieves. He tells me how Emmett gave his life serving the Lord playing banjo alongside his brother Enoch and Enoch's wife Margie, as the legendary Sullivan Family Gospel Singers. Jerry regarded Emmett a brother, and describes him as a "shade tree mechanic" who worked for whatever people would offer to pay him—a "love offering" in secular context. When Emmett died, his air conditioner and refrigerator were broken. Jerry says Emmett would do anything for people in need, and prays Emmett's friends and fellow churchgoers will contribute to Emmett's widow, Louise. Louise and Zelma had worked at Vanity Fair Mills in nearby Jackson. Zelma retired when pregnant with Stephanie in 1973. Today, Louise works at a Stop-N-Go store in Grove Hill.[2]

Jerry's countenance betrays a life lived hard hauling lumber from the woods with his father, driving trucks, working on oil rigs in the Gulf of Mexico, or traveling long, grueling miles singing gospel songs in the Deep South. At fifty-nine, his face is a complex interplay

"Jug's Jungle." Photo by Jack Bernhardt.

of kindness and pain. Years of laughter and sorrow have sculpted a visage of leathery features accented by a crooked nose broken as a child, he says, when the bus he rode in hit a pothole and he struck the seat in front. The nose was not set, and he has a blockage adding a slight nasality to his southwest Alabama drawl.

Jerry mentions his brother Arthur, who started the Sullivans on their gospel journey, and how Enoch and Margie accompanied Arthur to religious revivals, and on his radio and television ministry. Jerry animates his narrative with a wave of his hands, thick, strong appendages made muscular helping his father in the woods. As he speaks, his fingers twitch as if he's playing his guitar. Even subconsciously, music seems to pulse through him. When he gets tickled at a memory of an Emmett prank or a character he met at a church singing, Jerry lets go a belly laugh nearly as entertaining as the anecdote he shares.

The house is Zelma's world, her refuge when Jerry and Tammy are on the road. The grounds outside are a miniature botanical garden, planted by Zelma in an array of ornamental flowers, shrubs, and trees, interspersed with stone borders and yard art statuary. A front porch swing offers a breezy view of the leafy green canopy overarching the driveway leading to and from U.S. 43. Marty Stuart dubbed the verdant overhang, "Jug's Jungle." Jerry explains that nicknames are common in Washington County. Jerry is "Jug," or "Uncle Jug," coined by his nephew, Emmett, who also dubbed his brother, Enoch, "Jody." Tammy is "Hattie," after her paternal grandmother, and Jerry and Zelma call Stephanie, "Pudge," a carryover from her toddler years when, supposedly, she exhibited a "pudgy" nose. Former sheriff James Sullivan was "Peanut," and the inscription on George Washington Sullivan's (1887–1969) gravestone tells us he was known as "One-Eyed George."[3]

Tammy and Hanna drop by for a quick visit before disappearing into the office. Tammy serves as booking agent, finding names and phone numbers of pastors who have hired the Sullivans over the years, and new churches to contact for gigs. She knows most of the pastors personally, and tries to book tours that economize the cost of fuel. At venues, Tammy is road manager, ensuring the sound system is in place, along with other details to enable a successful concert. If she feels the responsibilities are burdensome, she doesn't complain.

Jerry wants to introduce me to his siblings, so after breakfast he and I visit his brother, Homer Lee, who lives up the road in a house trailer on ten acres he purchased from Arthur. Homer Lee, seventy-three, is an avid coon hunter who keeps ten well-bred hounds in a pen behind his trailer. Homer Lee is practicing for a fiddle contest he will enter two days from now. For his contest tunes, he's chosen "Cotton Patch Rag," an old warhorse in the key of C, and "Cruel Willie," a tune inspired by a moonshiner from Franklin, Tennessee. Homer Lee lays down his fiddle and plays a tape of North Carolina guitar legend, Doc Watson, playing and singing "Greenville Trestle High." "I just love that music," Homer Lee says. "And fox hounds and fishing."[4]

Vinyl records of Delia Bell and Bill Grant, Kenny Baker, Howdy Forrester, and other bluegrass artists lie scattered about the living room. A slingshot hangs by a nail on the living room wall. Fishing

Jerry and Homer Lee Sullivan jamming at home, Wagarville, Alabama. Photograph by Jack Bernhardt.

poles and a bucket of crickets repose next to the door, and three tackle boxes rest under the kitchen table. A grub fishing lure, milk bottle, white bread, and cereal share space on the table top. A guitar sits idle in its case, while another stretches across a living room chair. As Jerry and I prepare to leave, Vance Sullivan stops by. Son of Jerry's and Homer Lee's oldest brother, Dennis, Vance is in charge of the fiddler's convention. He will also play backup guitar for Homer Lee's performance on stage. Vance tells us the fiddler's convention originated in 1927 and is organized by the Masonic Lodge.

We depart Homer Lee's trailer and drive along County Road 34, "Mobile Cutoff Road," toward St. Stephens. Jerry points to a white frame house, home of Enoch and Margie Sullivan. Their new Silver Eagle bus is parked next to the road, its vivid green trim announcing The Legendary Sullivan Family. A second bus, bought years ago from bluegrass stars Jim and Jesse McReynolds, sits idle and a third, broken down and rusting, attests to the miles the family has traveled on its gospel journey.

Elva Sullivan Powell, Jerry's sister, Wagarville, Alabama.
Photograph by Jack Bernhardt.

The Sullivans' cattle graze in their pasture as Jerry motions to Arthur's house, abandoned now with years of neglect showing in its aged, gray siding. Across the road, the land is scarred from clear-cutting the longleaf pines important to the economy here. Random trees remain, interspersed with tall, blackened skeletons of tree trunks denuded of foliage on their gnarled branches. The scene emits an eerie feeling, as if an artillery barrage had taken place here.

Our last stop is a visit to Jerry's sister, Elva Sullivan Powell, who lives a few hundred yards behind Victory Grove Church. The Sullivans' home church, Victory Grove was built by Arthur Sullivan in 1949 and is pastored today by his youngest son, Arthur Glenn Sullivan. Jerry relies on Elva for spiritual and practical advice the way he had looked for guidance to Arthur. Wise and welcoming, Elva has been battling illness and Jerry and Brother Glenn include her in their prayers during services. Jerry values his visits with Elva, and fears he will struggle when she passes.

Ten years older than Jerry, Elva serves as family historian, sharing
stories of life during the Depression and the early years of Brother
Arthur's ministry. "My grandson asked me what we did when I was
growin' up. I said, 'We didn't have toys like y'all do. We had to make
ours.' I remember havin' such a good time 'cause I played with my
brothers. I was a tomboy. I would go with JB and Homer Lee whenever Papa would let us go in the woods with him when he was workin'. We'd find flowers. The boys would trap gophers and kill birds
with their slings. That's what I liked to do, whatever they done."

Even before Arthur's conversion in 1939, music was important in
the Sullivans' lives. It was partly because other forms of entertainment were scarce or nonexistent in their Washington County community. So they listened, played, and sang in the homes of family
members or friends, or in the churches nearby.

"Goin' to church and goin' to each other's houses was our pas-
time," Elva recalls. "On Saturday night, people would get together
and whoever could make music, that's what they done. Pick and
sing. And we'd listen to the Grand Ole Opry at our cousin's house.
There was a Free Holiness church down here. Me and Homer Lee
and some more kids would walk down here on the weekend and go
to church and sing. As soon as the singin' was over, we'd go home.
We had an aunt who would take us through the woods and across
the creek, and we'd walk about two miles to a Holiness church at
Mt. Nebo, and sing there."[5]

In the mid- to late 1930s, Elva and her siblings favored songs
they learned from the Carter Family and from Alabamians Alton
and Rabon Delmore, who performed and recorded as the Delmore
Brothers. The Carter Family hailed from southwest Virginia's Poor
Valley, and were among the most popular early country music
recording and radio acts. The Carters consisted of Alvin Pleasant
"A.P." Carter, his wife, Sarah, and A.P.'s sister-in-law Maybelle. A.P.
Carter traveled throughout the region selling fruit trees and collect-
ing songs he heard emanating from porches and parlors along the
way. Many of the songs found their way into Carter Family repertoire.

In 1927 the Carters along with Jimmie Rodgers and others answered a newspaper announcement inviting musicians to a recording session in nearby Bristol, Tennessee. Known as the "Bristol Sessions," it is regarded as a seminal event in the history of popular music and made stars of the Carters and Rodgers.

"What I remember about Brother Arthur's singing," Elva recalls, "he would always tell us he would 'A.P. it', which meant he was gonna sing bass. That's what we sung, the old Carter Family and Delmore Brothers songs. Me and Homer sung 'Sparkling Brown Eyes,' 'Weeping Willow'—them old-timey songs."[6]

When Arthur turned to religion and became a Pentecostal minister, he forsook secular music for gospel songs. Thus, the Sullivan Family began the career that would make them legends throughout the South and eventually earn them enshrinement in Bill Monroe's Bluegrass Hall of Fame Museum in Bean Blossom, Indiana.

We thank Elva for the visit, return to Jerry's house and dine on a bucket of Kentucky Fried Chicken. I settle in for the night on a bunk on the Sullivans' bus. It's been a good day and a good beginning to fieldwork. I feel welcomed by Jerry and Zelma, and look forward to adventures yet to unfold.

# Chapter 2

# The Sullivans of
# Washington County

Driving around southwest Alabama's Washington County, one may imagine the gently rolling landscape of pine and pasture is God's country, or at least that God has some special interest here. Turn your radio on and you have the choice of listening to gospel music, hellfire preaching, or politically charged evangelical talk shows on AM and FM stations up and down the dial. One show's sponsor, a local laundry, offers pastors a 10 percent discount on dry cleaning.

Well-groomed pastors minister in an impressive array of churches representing Baptist, Missionary Baptist, United Methodist, Holiness, A.M.E. Zion, Church of God, Pentecostal, and other denominations standing stout beside major thoroughfares or tucked away in shady groves along dusty side roads. As you approach the county seat on Highway 56, you're greeted by a brick monument at the town line that reads, "Welcome to Chatom. In God We Trust." The American Civil Liberties Union, crusaders for the separation of church and state, does not have a foothold in Washington County.

Even the first capital of Alabama bore the name of a religious figure. St. Stephens, established by the Spanish as Fort San Esteban on the banks of the Tombigbee River, became the seat of government

of the Alabama Territory in 1817. The Territory's first church was
located here. Sharing a building with a theater company, it was an
early example of the Saturday night/Sunday morning dichotomy
condemned by pastors and embraced by members of their congregations. A visitor to St. Stephens in 1818 described the town as
consisting of "300 to 350 houses & from 1500 to 2000 inhabitants,
several taverns—35, by one account—and stores, & one church
which is likewise used occasionally for a theater. It is reputed very
healthy, the water is impregnated with lime, & the river water, when
filtered, is not unpalatable."[1]

According to legend, a Methodist circuit rider was so appalled by
the debauchery he witnessed that he visited taverns on the Sabbath
and railed against the residents for their sinful ways. The patrons
responded by tarring and feathering the hapless evangelist and setting him afloat on a raft. As he drifted from shore, the minister
screamed his prophesy that bats and owls would descend on the
town, and pestilence would destroy the settlement. Some years later,
a yellow fever epidemic killed a significant number of inhabitants
and forced others to leave their homes. The epidemic is thought by
some to have prompted abandonment of Old St. Stephens, which
was a virtual ghost town at the beginning of the Civil War.[2]

The first Sullivans arrived in Washington County from the
Carolinas around the turn of nineteenth century. Owen Sullivan
settled here between 1790 and 1800 with a Spanish grant of 400
acres on a creek north of Three Rivers Lake. Jerry Sullivan and his
family trace their immediate lineage to Jerry's great-grandfather,
Gibeon "Grandpa Gib" Sullivan (1831–1914). Gibeon's cabin, built on
the east side of Bassett Creek near Wagarville in 1874, is the oldest
remaining example of domestic architecture in Washington County,
and is believed to be the second-oldest home in Alabama. Today,
the house sits silent, surrounded by weeds. But marble gravestones
in the family burial ground behind the house announce the names
of three early residents: Con Sullivan (1788–1860), Mark Sullivan
(1790–1859), Buck Sullivan (1839–1859).[3]

Gibeon served as color bearer of Company A, 32nd Alabama Regiment. On December 16, 1864, Gib was taken prisoner at the battle of Nashville, Tennessee, and incarcerated at Camp Chase, the Federal prison camp at Columbus, Ohio. At war's end, he walked home carrying his captain's ailing son across streams and reunited with his wife and children at the tiny Washington County community of St. Stephens. There he built his four-bedroom, dog-trot style log home with hand-hewn timbers cut from the surrounding forest. In 1874, he nailed three planks together to fashion a "cooling board," upon which were laid recently deceased members of the community as they were prepared for burial. The cooling board, which today sits idle on Gibeon's front porch, made the Sullivan home an important center of community involvement as neighbors would gather to pay respects and give and receive comfort in their time of grief.[4]

Jerry Sullivan is the second-youngest of twelve children born to J.B. Sullivan and Hattie Knapp. Three Sullivan children died young: their son, J.B., was a victim of the flu pandemic of 1918–19, and twins Harroll and Carroll lived only one week in 1922. Born in 1913, the second-eldest child, Arthur, would grow up to play a central role in the Sullivan family's religious and musical lives.

The Sullivan family was not actively religious when Jerry was a boy. J.B. and Hattie were on the rolls of Clearwater Baptist Church, but the demands of work and raising nine surviving children didn't leave much time for religion or other activities outside the home. A lumber contractor by trade, J.B. trekked to the piney woods six days a week, cutting timber and hauling it out on ox-drawn wagons to trains waiting to transport the logs to saw and pulp mills near Mobile.

In *Logging Roads of Alabama*, railroad historian Thomas Lawson Jr. conveys that the Alabama timber industry "was established during Reconstruction, following the Civil War. It expanded rapidly in the 1880s. The most efficient means of transport was by rail, rather than floating logs downstream as previously done.

"Over flimsy rails, hastily spiked to freshly-cut road ties laid in a sandy clay roadbed, came the log train with its clanging rods, groaning wheels and clouds of steam and smoke. Across creaking wooden trestles, up steep grades and around tight curves, no virgin forest was safe from its relentless path.

"Logging was done by hand. Two-man crosscut saws and axes were the primary tools. Once felled, the 500-year-old trees were dragged by ox or mule teams to a spur line branching out into the wilderness from the main tracks leading back to the sawmill."[5]

The Sullivans divided their time between their two-room house near St. Stephens and the lumber camps that housed, fed, and employed gangs of workers in large-scale projects requiring a concentrated, temporary labor force. While her husband was in the woods, Hattie looked after the children and cooked meals for the men, who returned tired and hungry at the end of the day.

The Sullivans' walk with God came about, as conversions often do, at a time of crisis. The second-born son, Arthur was afflicted with a congenital heart defect that resulted in occasional blackouts and periods of unconsciousness. At age twenty-six in 1939, he suffered a heart attack and lapsed into a coma. Arriving at the Sullivans' home by horse and buggy, a local doctor examined Arthur and informed the family that it was not likely Arthur would emerge from the coma, and that his death was imminent. Hearing the news of Arthur's illness, two Holiness preachers from nearby St. Stephens walked four miles to the Sullivans' home to hold a prayer vigil. Arthur also received the prayers of Mr. Clarence Johnson and his wife, Nancy, who, Jerry recalls, arrived at the house on the back of a large black stallion. Jerry describes Mrs. Johnson as "a tongue-talking holiness believer" who, throughout the night, went in and out of speaking in tongues. Mrs. Johnson's glossolalia alarmed Arthur's father-in-law, who did not understand that aspect of faith and was certain God would strike them all dead. Jerry recalls how he and Arthur's son Enoch sat in an adjoining room listening apprehensively to the visitors moan their incantations in the eerie darkness as they knelt beside Arthur's bed.

"I remember bein' frightened at them prayin'," Jerry says, animating his story with wavering hands. "Me and my nephew Enoch,

Arthur's son, listened to 'em. The next day, Arthur woke up. The doctor had said that he may not know anything if he *did* wake up. But he did. He woke up and he was just ready to go on with his life. God just raised him up, and he begin to think about Christianity and what these men had prayed for, and he changed his life completely."[6]

Believing he had been spared from death through the prayers of his neighbors, Arthur committed himself to doing the Lord's work. After regaining his strength, he constructed a brush arbor in a vacant lot near a curve of the Mobile cut-off road, about a half-mile from his house. Arthur invited traveling preachers to hold revivals and Sunday worship services at the arbor, and to care for the spiritual welfare of his family and community.

In the annals of the Sullivan family's spiritual quest, no memory holds greater meaning than the brush arbor. It was here that the family began its spiritual journey and sounded the first chords of its lifelong commitment to musical ministry. The Sullivans incorporate songs about brush arbors into their repertoires, and Jerry Sullivan frequently speaks of his brush arbor experiences in concert. His composition, "Old Brush Arbor Meetings" appears on Jerry and Tammy Sullivan's 1981 album *The Old Home Place*.[7] In areas of the South that were poor or so sparse in population that permanent church buildings were neither practical nor affordable, the brush arbor served as a temporary gathering place for revivals and prayer.

Margie Louise Brewster Sullivan is the sixth of twelve children born to a Louisiana sharecropper and his wife. Margie recalls attending a brush arbor revival in Baskin, Louisiana. She played guitar and sang gospel songs with her family. In 1946 thirteen-year-old Margie left home to accompany traveling evangelist Hazel Chain. Sister Hazel preached, and Margie strummed the guitar and sang. She met Jerry's nephew, Enoch Sullivan, at a revival in southwest Alabama. She was thirteen and Enoch fifteen. They married in 1949.[8]

Constructed from poles cut from the surrounding forests and roofed with hastily gathered bunches of branches and brush, these rustic rural temples offered refuge from the sun's oppressive heat

Enoch and Margie Sullivan, Redbud Festival, Saxapahaw, NC, 2005. Photograph by Jack Bernhardt.

while worshippers gathered to praise the Lord. Inside, the congregation welcomed the caress of whatever breeze might waft across the pews, which were no more substantial than rough-hewn planks nailed to sections of short log posts set at intervals in the ground. Jerry recalls how Arthur and his family and friends cut down trees to build a frame that measured some fifteen by twenty feet on a side.

"They would take smaller trees and nail them or wire them to the tops of the posts. They would run those across the top for rafters. Then the people would cut bushes and they would pile the brush on top of the rafters. It was a humble place that wouldn't keep out the rain or snow, but it would keep out the sun so that people could gather to talk about Jesus and sing and have a wonderful time. They didn't have electricity so people would hang a coal oil lamp, and people would come in wagons drawn by mules or horses or oxen. That's how I came to know the Lord in my Christian walk, at a brush arbor meeting when I was a boy.

"A preacher would come and stay with us for two, three, or four weeks, or even longer. An eight-week revival wasn't too much. Lookin' back over it, I can remember how it looked—there must have been anywhere from thirty to sixty or seventy people. I remember these people who came from Hobson on a flatbed truck. They had maybe twenty-five people on one truck. The whole community would load up and come. You wouldn't see too many automobiles, but you'd see one or two of these flatbed trucks and the rest of it was mules and wagons and buckboards, things like that. But there was one family from Jackson. They were barbers—that's where my dad would go to get his hair cut. They would come and they would be in an automobile. They would drive past [the brush arbor]. They wouldn't get up where they would get under the spell of that thing, but they'd want to hear the singin', and they would come and listen."[9]

If Brother Arthur is the Sullivan family's St. Peter, the brush arbor is the "rock" upon which he built his church. It is almost always referenced in their testimony and memorialized in song. Their brush arbor origins confer legitimacy upon the family, grounding them in the "old-time religion" and authenticating their ministry by connecting it to the Old South's nineteenth-century agrarian values. Importantly, it allies them through Brother Arthur with old-time circuit-riding evangelists rather than to Jim and Tammy Faye Bakker or Jimmy Swaggart and other fallen angels of the electronic church. For Margie Sullivan and Enoch and Jerry, who came of age spiritually through Brother Arthur, the brush arbor holds deeply ingrained, personal meanings. One of Margie's most popular songs remains "Old Brush Arbors," an old-time gospel celebration recorded by the great country singer, George Jones.

"He Called My Name," which Jerry wrote with Marty Stuart, recalls the sultry summer evening in 1944 when Jerry, then ten years old, made his first altar call:

> While walking down a country road praises filled the air
> From the old brush arbor, many souls were gathered there
> A feeling deep inside me like a burning flame
> As I drew near I could hear the Savior call my name
>
> CHORUS: He called my name, He called my name
> His voice I heard so plain

He took away the guilt and shame
Praise the Lord, He called my name

They gathered all around me as I was kneeling there
It seemed a thousand angels came and took my prayer
Heaven's gates were opened, victory I could claim
My name was added to the book the night He called my name[10]

As more people attended the brush arbor services, the community recognized the need for a permanent structure. Arthur, family members, friends, and neighbors built Cedar Curve Church of God on the spot of the original brush arbor. Built on land donated by Mr. and Mrs. H. L. Powell and incorporating logs provided by Jerry's father and grandfather, the church measured 16 × 20 feet, and was dedicated on St. Patrick's Day.[11] At the end of the decade, the building was torn down and another, more permanent structure built in its place. The newer church remains active today and is attended by a community of old-time Holiness worshippers, the spiritual descendants of the preachers who prayed for Arthur's relief from coma and return to health.

Arthur had no formal theological training, but learned to preach by observing and talking with evangelists who held revivals and other services at the brush arbor and at Cedar Curve Church. Assisted by members of his family and friends, Arthur built Victory Grove Church in 1949. The modest rectangular frame building sits beside US Highway 43, designated the Jefferson Davis Highway, named for the president of the Confederate States of America. Today, Victory Grove is led by Arthur's son, the Reverend Glenn Sullivan.

Arthur was licensed to the ministry of the Assemblies of the Lord Jesus Christ, a denomination of Pentecostal believers that branched off from the larger Assemblies of God in 1917.[12] What sets these worshippers apart from other Pentecostals is their disavowal of the Trinity in favor of a belief in Jesus as the sole figure of the Godhead. Called by various names, including "Oneness Pentecostals," "Jesus Only," "Jesus Name," and "Unitarian

Victory Grove Church, Wagarville, Alabama. Photograph by Jack Bernhardt.

Pentecostals," their Christocentrism is based on their interpretation of Acts 2:38, which reads, "Then Peter said unto them, Repent,
and be baptized every one of you in the name of Jesus Christ
for the remission of sins, and ye shall receive the gift of the Holy
Ghost." Thus, the name "Jesus Christ" is seen to be the singularly
revealed name of the Father, Son, and Holy Spirit. Religious scholar
H. Richard Niebuhr calls this worship "practical monotheism of
the Son," and says, "such expressions are not indeed necessarily
exclusive of devotion to the Father and the Spirit, but practically
the whole thought about God is concentrated here in the thought
about the Son; he is the sole object of worship and all the functions
of deity are ascribed to him."[13]

Generally, those who chose Jesus Only worship were of lower
socioeconomic status than their Trinitarian counterparts. Initially,
nearly half of all Unitarians were Black, but by the late 1930s the
movement had segregated along racial lines. By this time, the total
Oneness Pentecostal membership numbered 31,464, with only
1,970 members living within the east south-central region of the
United States, which included Mississippi and Alabama. Today, their
churches are scattered throughout the United States, but concentrate
in areas of the Midwest, such as southern Indiana and south and
central Missouri, where folklorist Elaine Lawless did her research
on Oneness Pentecostal women in the 1980s.[14]

As a licensing body, the Assemblies of the Lord Jesus Christ formulated a catalog of rules dictating rigid codes of conduct, dress, and grooming for its members. Jerry Sullivan characterizes these proscriptions as "walk right and spit white," a metaphor referencing the Assemblies' prohibition on the use of intoxicants, chewing tobacco, and snuff. Brother Arthur determined that these restrictions interfered with the goals of his ministry and he minimized their importance while continuing to follow and preach Unitarian theology. Ironically, many of these same rules caused schisms to develop within Victory Grove Church as recently as the 1980s and '90s.

By all accounts, Brother Arthur was a thoughtful, charming, charismatic personality whose counsel was sought by those seeking relief from burdens great or small. As second-eldest son, he relished the role of big brother, offering guidance and comfort to his younger siblings. "Even before he called himself a preacher, he was a person who could give you hope," Jerry says. "If you had a problem, he would say, 'Let me tell you how to fix that,' and you would feel so much better after you talked to him. He just had a way he could touch you—put his hand on your shoulder. When I was a little fella, I would worry about things. He would lower his voice real quiet and say, 'Don't worry about that. Come let Brother Arthur talk to you a minute about that, and then you won't be worried about it no more.' I miss it so much now."[15]

It was Arthur, too, who encouraged his family to learn music to accompany him at church services and revivals, and to help attract crowds for his street-corner preaching. Even before Arthur's conversion, the banjo had provided homegrown entertainment on many summer evenings on the family's front porch. Jerry's father, J.B. Sullivan, was an accomplished banjoist who played in the old-time clawhammer, or drop thumb, style. In this style, which preceded the innovations of Earl Scruggs and other bluegrass banjoists,[16] the musician can pick out melodies to such ancient favorites as "Old Joe Clark," "Cumberland Gap," and "Flop-Eared Mule" while creating percussive, drum-like rhythms. His father's banjo playing on the front porch is one of Jerry's warmest childhood memories. Jerry remembers that his father's banjo picking "gave the music a far-off, lonesome sound, like the soft, sad echo of a cry in the forest. I couldn't wait 'til Saturday night," he says. "That was our entertainment for the week. He worked all week and would take the banjo on Saturday night and he would play for us. Then, he'd take us fox huntin'. That was the two things I looked forward to."[17]

The Sullivans were a musical family, playing and singing the old-time songs popularized by the Grand Ole Opry radio broadcasts or by 78 rpm recordings made by country music artists of the 1920s and '30s. Jerry's father learned to play banjo from Alec Eason, a Black man who lived nearby in the "colored" section, and the family also had a small collection of 78 rpm recordings. Each of Jerry's siblings played musical instruments or sang. Jerry's nephew, Enoch, began playing guitar at the age of eight; two years later, Arthur traded a pig for a fiddle, and Enoch began his lifelong involvement with the instrument known as "the devil's box." Enoch was especially fond of his father's 78 rpm recordings of Mainer's Mountaineers and the Georgia Wildcats, two energetic string bands whose recordings in the 1920s and '30s emphasized the role of the fiddle.[18]

At about the same age, Jerry began playing guitar. In the early years, gospel music was one of, but by no means the major, focus of the Sullivan family's musical interests. Jerry was influenced by Big Joe Turner, Jimmy Reed, and other blues musicians, and would record and perform rockabilly songs in the early 1950s. But after his brush arbor conversion, Arthur encouraged the family to shun secular "frolic" music, which was often associated with rowdy, alcohol-fueled square dances, and asked them to learn gospel songs to accompany his preaching. Although the fiddle was regarded by some church people as "the devil's box," Brother Arthur assured his followers that it would not do the devil's work. Sullivan Family fiddler Enoch recalls his struggles early in his career convincing churchgoers the fiddle could do the Lord's work as well as the devil's:

Revival ca. 1948. L-r: Arthur Sullivan, Jerry Sullivan, Enoch Sullivan. Photograph courtesy of Tammy Sullivan.

"When you walked into the church with a fiddle, somebody would start the hillbilly holler—'Yee-haw!'—you know. It was comical to them. They said the fiddle was the devil's instrument, which was an old-time sayin' because the women didn't like for the men to go off and stay out all night. They'd say, 'The devil's in the fiddle. He'd stay out all night with that thing. He loves it better than he loves me.' But the good Lord helped me to come up with a lighthearted way to put it. I'd always say, 'First, you gotta get the devil outta the fiddler, then the fiddle's as sacred as he makes it.'"[19]

Although less accomplished on his instrument, Brother Arthur set the tone for the family ministry by establishing rhythms that mimicked the cadence of his old-time preaching style. "Arthur played the mandolin, and he would lead the choir and play rhythm with it," Jerry recalls. "Then he'd get up and sing and we'd all really learn from that. And a lot of times we didn't have music. They'd sort of slap their hands and sing. That's why our rhythm is like it is. We have sort of a different rhythm. . . . It come from south Alabama and Mississippi from the Pentecostal people. They sung shoutin' songs and they'd pat their hands and tap their feet, and some times that was the only musical instruments they had. But it made for some beautiful singin'. That kind of singin' is what touched my life as a very young person and turned my whole life around."[20]

Music and the ecstatic vocal expression of "shouting" are essential components of Pentecostal worship, finding Scriptural authority in the Book of Psalms. Psalm 95 invites the worshipper: "Come, let us sing for joy to the Lord; Let us shout aloud to the Rock of our salvation. Let us come before Him with thanksgiving and extol Him with music and song." And, in perhaps the most famous musical passage in the Bible, Psalm 100 exhorts the faithful to "Make a joyful noise unto the Lord, all ye lands. Serve the Lord with gladness: come before His presence with singing."

The invitation to "make a joyful noise" has opened the doors to unlimited choices of melody and instruments to accompany singing in both Black and White Holiness and Pentecostal churches. It is not uncommon to hear singers accompanied by the amalgamated sounds of drums, tambourines, handclaps, guitars, trumpets, washtub bass, piano, and whatever else is available and considered appropriate within the traditions of individual churches. Brother Arthur Sullivan followed the Holiness tradition by encouraging his family to learn to play instruments donated by members of the church. While all members of the family joined in from time to time, Jerry, his brothers Homer and Aubrey, and his sister Suzie, and their nephews Enoch and Emmett were especially active at an early age, accompanying Arthur on his travels through the region. With Arthur on mandolin, Margie on guitar, Enoch on fiddle, and Arthur's

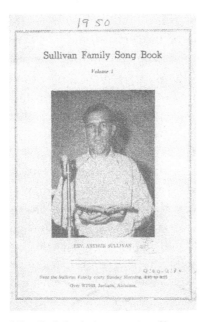

Sullivan Family Songbook, 1950, courtesy of Tammy
Sullivan. Photograph by Jack Bernhardt.

brother, Aubry, on guitar, the Sullivans performed their first radio
broadcast on WRJW in Picayune, Mississippi, on December 23, 1949.
Enoch and Margie regard this date as the beginning of the Sullivan
Family's professional career.[21] Within two months, they were offered
a second radio broadcast on newly commissioned WPBB in Jackson,
Alabama, and the family's popularity began to spread throughout
Alabama and Mississippi as folks tuned in each Sunday morning to
hear Arthur's fiery sermons and the family's old-time gospel songs.

It was also in 1949 that Arthur Sullivan built Victory Grove
Church in Wagarville, pastored today by Jerry's nephew, Glenn
Sullivan. While the doctrine of the Assemblies sets Oneness
Pentecostals apart from their Trinitarian counterparts and marks
them as a minority branch of Christianity, it does not appear to
influence the way the Sullivans conduct their lives or compose their
gospel songs, which are ecumenical in their messages. Encouraged

by Arthur, several members of the Sullivan family learned to sing and to play acoustic instruments, and they often accompanied Arthur at street preaching, revivals, church services, and Sunday radio broadcasts. In 1953 Arthur built a second church, Bolentown Jesus Name Pentecostal Church, in neighboring Clarke County.

On Thanksgiving weekend 1957, Arthur was preaching from the pulpit of the Bolentown church when he suffered a heart attack and died.[22] "He wouldn't have wanted to go any other way," says Margie Sullivan, who was in church with the family on that day. "He was so sold out to the Gospel and to the ministry." Arthur's work and death are celebrated in "Sing Daddy a Song," one of the family's most cherished compositions, written by Jerry Sullivan in 1961.[23] Arthur was Jerry's sibling, but with a twenty-year difference in their ages, Jerry regarded Arthur as his "spiritual father." Arthur is celebrated in family lore and is honored with the song's performance at the family's homecomings, held each Easter Sunday at Victory Grove Church:

Chorus
Let's sing a song for Daddy
He left us a long time ago
Though it broke our hearts when God called him
He's happy in Heaven I know
His parting words when he left us, "Remember us when I
     am gone
When you have a family reunion, please sing Daddy a song"

Before Daddy died he taught us
Many gospel songs that we sing
And under God's great inspiration
My how his voice would ring
He never grew tired of helping
Or correcting us when we were wrong
When you have a family reunion
Please sing Daddy a song

Chorus

(Jerry, spoken/chanted) He was workin' so hard when God
    called him
Tryin' to prepare the way
For us children to sing for Jesus
Til we leave here and join him one day
He died while preaching a sermon
Tellin' the sinful to turn from their wrongs
A great man of God, our Daddy
And we proudly dedicate him this song

Chorus

Following Arthur's death, the Sullivan Family Gospel Singers continued their musical ministry, traveling the back roads and serving
the backwoods churches from the Florida Panhandle to East Texas
and beyond. The core band consisted of Arthur's sons Emmett and
Enoch, along with Enoch's wife Margie, although it often featured
other musicians, including Joe Cook, Carl Jackson, Marty Stuart,
Jerry, and Jerry's brother Aubrey and sister Suzie.

Jerry had played in bluegrass, rockabilly, and rhythm and blues
bands and served a two-year hitch in the army before rejoining the
Sullivan Family in the late 1950s. He wrote songs and played bass
with the Sullivan Family until 1977, when a near-fatal traffic accident
forced him to discontinue his travels with the band. Two years later,
Jerry and his thirteen-year-old daughter Tammy, whose singing
style echoed Margie's old-time gospel sound, began their career
together following the model of backwoods ministry Jerry's family
had known for more than thirty years. This formed the foundation
of Jerry and Tammy Sullivan's ministry from its beginning in 1979
until Jerry's death in 2014.

# Chapter 3

# Serve the Lord with Gladness
## *Make a Joyful Noise*

In faith communities of the American South, gospel music is among the most significant artistic expressions of Christian values and worldview.[1] Affirming a personal or collective embrace of Protestant beliefs, gospel music permeates working- and middle-class culture, from religious ceremonialism and personal enrichment to popular entertainments and the commercialism of the recording and broadcast industries.

With origins in early nineteenth-century camp-meeting songs, shape-note singing, and brush arbor revivals, the gospel music industry emerged in the decades after the Civil War. Publishing companies, such as Ruebush-Kieffer in Virginia's Shenandoah Valley, popularized sacred singing by issuing songbooks using the newly developed seven-shape system for representing different notes. The seven-shape system supplanted the four-shape notation of the earlier Sacred Harp formulation, expanding the musical possibilities of gospel songs. In 1875 northerners Ira D. Sankey and Philip P. Bliss published *Gospel Hymns and Sacred Tunes*, a songbook that embedded lyrics within arrangements inspired from the popular songs of the day. Aimed at bringing young people into the church, the Sankey

Shape Note Hymnal. Photograph by Jack Bernhardt.

and Bliss hymns became the principal template for gospel songs well into the twentieth century.

The popularity of the new songs spread quickly, as Ruebush Kieffer and other publishers hired singing teachers to conduct singing schools throughout the rural South. Armed with songbooks published by their employers and proficient in shape-note (also known as "shaped note") technique, singing school teachers lived an itinerant lifestyle, moving from community to community and holding ten-day singing schools for rural residents during the months before autumn harvests. Holding forth in one-room schoolhouses or other available spaces, these teachers taught songs published in their employers' songbooks, popularizing the songs and generating profits by creating a market for the books. Well into the twentieth century, singing schools were an important means by which gospel songs entered into individual and congregational repertoires, from North Carolina's coastal plain to Arkansas's rugged Ozark Mountains. Jerry Sullivan recalls a singing school held at Cedar Curve Holiness Church between Wagarville and St. Stephens. Many shape-note songs, "Precious Memories," "Leaning on the Everlasting Arms," and "Rank Stranger to Me," among them, remain popular today.

In 1902 James D. Vaughan, a former singing school teacher from Tennessee, founded the Vaughan Publishing Company, which he promoted by means of singing schools, a monthly magazine (*Vaughan's Family Visitor*), and professional quartets that toured the South performing Vaughan's songs. By 1921 Vaughan had added a record company to his publishing enterprise; two years later, he founded his own radio station, Lawrenceburg, Tennessee's WOAN. Vaughan's radio venture followed Atlanta's WSB (1922), the first radio station to broadcast in the South. These and other stations, including WBAP in Fort Worth, Texas (1922), and Nashville, Tennessee's WSM (1925), aired live performances that featured both secular and sacred programs. As more radio stations and record companies opened throughout the region, gospel music became one of the South's most important expressions of entertainment and faith.[2]

In the twenty-first century, gospel continues to evolve, adapting to changing musical tastes. Today, it is heard in a variety of styles, from bluegrass to honky-tonk and contemporary country; smooth, piano- and organ-backed Southern gospel; lushly orchestrated praise music; and heavy metal Christian rock. Especially popular among White churchgoers, Southern gospel is sometimes known as "quartet music" because of its origins as all-male, tenor/lead/baritone/bass vocal quartets.[3] Early examples included Smith's Sacred Singers, the Stamps Quartet, and the Speer Family. Today, Southern gospel is represented by Gold City, the Calvarymen, the Gaither Vocal Band, and others, as well as such female-featured groups as the Isaacs and the Happy Goodman Family. Still, its core rests in Southern folk traditions as an integral part of the lives of individuals, families, and communities throughout the South.

Each week, thousands of churches, from tiny backwoods sanctuaries to urban brick-and-glass cathedrals, incorporate gospel songs into their services. Drawing guidance from the Book of Psalms, "O come, let us sing unto the Lord: let us make a joyful noise to the rock of our salvation," many churches feature musicians who are members of the congregation and who accompany services with traditional and original songs. These amateur musicians play a variety of instruments, from pianos to fiddles, banjos, guitars, mandolins, tambourines, drums, and electric and upright basses.

Many Southern congregations rely on songbooks that feature conventional music notation; one familiar favorite is *The American Service Hymnal: A Collection of the Great Hymns and Gospel Songs, New and Old, Whose Melodies and Truths Will Meet the Needs of All Churches.* Other churches use books that symbolically feature the seven-shape note system established in the nineteenth century. For example, *Great Gospel Hymns, Number 3 (Shaped Notes Only),* compiled by O. C. Thompson of Pineville, Louisiana, includes such standards as "The Old Country Church," "Where the Soul Never Dies," "Old Time Power," "I'll Fly Away," and the Stamps Quartet's 1948 composition, "What a Savior." The cover of this volume, published in

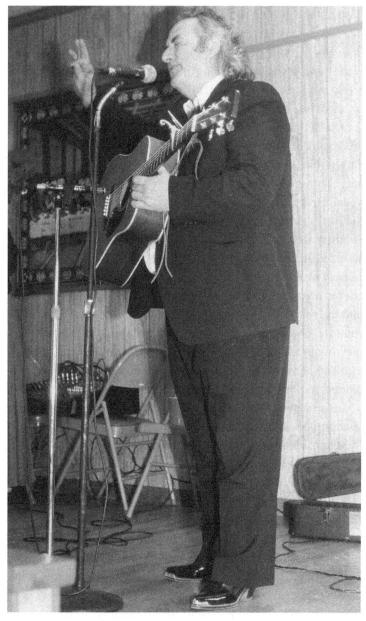

Jerry Sullivan testifying, Church of the Lord Jesus, Goodway, Alabama. Photograph by Jack Bernhardt.

1979, is inscribed with the notation, "If you are in need of a singing school in your church or community, write: O. C. Thompson." The continuing preference for the classics and shape-note representations connects today's worshippers with their ancestors and the old-time religion, grounding them in tangible family and community traditions of song and style.

Gospel music plays an equally important role outside the church. Its performance at homecomings and fundraisers, at music festivals and gospel concerts, and on local radio and television broadcasts affirms the spiritual identity of the community and promotes a bond of belief and belonging, or *communitas*,[4] among the faithful. While written primarily to offer praise or give thanks to God, gospel songs often embody multiple meanings, some of which may resonate with the needs or experiences of the listener, while others may carry broader meanings embedded in community history and tradition.[5]

Songs such as Albert Brumley's "I'll Fly Away" and Jerry Sullivan's "Born Again Experience" celebrate personal salvation and belief in the heavenly reward. Others have topical themes that address issues of concern to local communities. Early Grand Ole Opry star Uncle Dave Macon, for example, recorded "The Bible's True" as anti-evolutionary commentary on the Scopes "Monkey" Trial of 1925: "God made the world and everything that's in it / He made man perfect and the monkey wasn't in it." In 1962 northern Alabama's Louvin Brothers expressed concern over US Supreme Court rulings concerning separation of church and state with "Don't Let Them Take the Bible Out of Our School Rooms." While of national consequence, these events resonated across the South with families worried their children would be exposed to Darwinism or other secularizing ideas in the public schools. Jerry Sullivan's "Shadow of the Steeple," written in 2007, exhorts worshippers to open their eyes and hearts to those who make their homes in cardboard boxes and decaying doorways within view of the stained-glass opulence of Sunday services.

In the American South, musical ministries have long been among the most popular means for sharing new and old gospel songs with

Southern audiences. Family-centered gospel groups have a long legacy in the region, and include such heralded acts as the Isaacs, Chuck Wagon Gang, Joel and LaBreeska Hemphill, the Rambos, Joe Cook family, and the Happy Goodmans. Led by Enoch and Margie Sullivan, the Sullivan Family Gospel Singers performed bluegrass gospel exclusively since 1949. The Sullivans, Georgia's Lewis Family, and countless others are inspired by the music of the late Kentuckian Bill Monroe, who made gospel an integral part of the bluegrass music he developed between 1938 and 1945.[6] These musical evangelists take their songs and testimonies to churches, camp-meetings, tent revivals, and festivals, both sacred and secular, presenting their music as religious vocation and a means for earning a livelihood.

In the rural South, many churches are small, consisting of twenty or fewer, generally elderly, members; the children and grandchildren of today's congregants have often moved to cities providing opportunities for employment and entertainment unavailable in rural regions. Singing evangelists commonly perform at these churches for "love offerings," voluntary "pass-the-plate" donations from audience members of limited income, often supplemented by a stipend offered by the pastor. Both entertaining and faith-affirming, these gospel singings also may feature and validate the talents of church members who perform and testify during intermissions.

Throughout the South, local and national television broadcasts, AM and FM radio stations, and internet streaming transmit gospel music into homes, automobiles, and business establishments.[7] Television shows—Bill and Gloria Gaither's *Gaither Gospel Hour* on the GAC network, for example—or specials, such as *Silent Witness*, hosted by Grand Ole Opry star Ricky Skaggs, combine testimonies and music from notable guests whose numbers included Johnny Cash, Tammy Wynette, Glen Campbell, Dolly Parton, Marty Stuart, and Jerry and Tammy Sullivan.[8]

In addition to airing a wide range of gospel music styles, religious radio stations often broadcast church services and sermons, provide important information on farm and industry news, make public service announcements, and report on the health and welfare of members of the community. *The Radio Book*, a broadcast yearbook published by M Street Publications, reports a total of 322 Southern Gospel radio stations in July 2008; it lists an additional 37 stations as "gospel," 936 as Contemporary Christian, and 1,269 as following a Religion (Teaching/Variety) format.

The importance of gospel music to White Southerners is further witnessed in the fact that most bluegrass and country artists include religious songs in their repertoires, and that many have recorded entire albums of gospel songs. Popular bluegrass artists Ralph Stanley, Ricky Skaggs, and Doyle Lawson, for instance, have made gospel music a regular feature of their recordings and stage shows, and its welcomed performance at festivals and in concert draws loud and sustained applause. Blending Southern gospel vocals with bluegrass instrumentation, North Carolina's Primitive Quartet merges sacred music with patriotism during their annual Singing in Hominy Valley festival, held near Asheville over the Fourth of July weekend. The Primitives describe their music as "the traditional mountain shape note style singing accompanied by acoustical instruments including the mandolin, banjo, fiddle, guitars and acoustic bass."[9]

Southerners young and old may also connect with gospel sentiments through recordings and performances by their favorite country artists. Country music stars Charlie Daniels and Brad Paisley, for example, often include a gospel number or two on their secular albums. Others, including Elvis Presley, Dolly Parton, Hank Williams, Loretta Lynn, Johnny Cash, and Alan Jackson, have recorded all-gospel albums, reminding fans of their shared cultural connections and proclaiming commitment to evangelical beliefs.

Many country music stars also construct songs aimed at the secular market around gospel sentiments; a host of such pieces became popular hits. Randy Travis's "Forever and Ever Amen," a musical affirmation of everlasting love, helped launch his career when it was released as the first single from his second LP, *Always and Forever*, in 1987. Carrie Underwood, star of television's popular *American Idol*, enjoyed enormous success in 2006 with her chart-topping prayer-song, "Jesus Take the Wheel." And the following year, Martina McBride scored a top-five hit with "Anyway," a song praising God's greatness and invoking the power of prayer.

From modest beginnings in shape-note hymnals and brush arbor revivals, gospel music has evolved in response to changing historical trends, song styles, and technology. Regardless of form or function, it remains grounded in Southern folk tradition, drawing upon a common Protestant heritage expressed through shared cultural symbols of faith and through songs that celebrate family, salvation, and the infinite goodness of God. For Southerners, gospel music remains one of the most popular expressions of faith and virtue. Its diverse strains continue to be heard in homes and churches, on radio and television, and at sacred and secular gatherings throughout and beyond the South.

*Chapter 4*

# Love and Loss and the High Lonesome Sound

The moment he heard Lougenia sing, Jerry Sullivan knew he'd found his dream girl. It was a sultry summer evening in 1947, and Lougenia had accompanied her mother and sister to a revival in a private home in Sunflower, seven miles south of Wagarville. Lougenia's mother, a self-professed Holiness evangelist, played piano and preached the gospel while Lougenia and her sister Eulie, performed together as the Johnson Sisters, harmonizing the old hymns. Originally from south Georgia, the Johnsons had evangelized in Miami before heading out on the revival circuit that brought them into the Sullivans' world.

Each evening, with chores and work in the woods behind them, Jerry and other members of his family trekked to Sunflower to sing and fellowship with the evangelists and their followers. Lougenia sang with a sweet, old-timey Southern twang that blended perfectly with Jerry's resonant baritone. As the weeks passed, their mutual fondness for gospel duets blossomed into romance. To the son of a hard-working lumberman, the prospect of singing and playing guitar at revivals alongside pretty Lougenia must have seemed heavenly compared to toiling in the hot, humid woods of Washington County.

Jerry Sullivan and his sister Susie, ca. 1947. Wagarville, Alabama. Photograph courtesy of Tammy Sullivan.

When the Johnsons left Sunflower for Miami, Jerry left with them. Passing through Douglas, Georgia, they tracked down a justice of the peace, convinced her Jerry was twenty-one years old, and he and Lougenia married. Lougenia was eighteen; Jerry, who looked mature for his age, was fourteen. "I just walked up to a lady justice and told her I wanted to get married," Jerry recalls. "She fixed me a license and fixed my age on it like I was twenty-one years old."[1]

The newlyweds settled in Plant City, Florida, where Jerry found a job working at a sausage factory. Lougenia's stepfather, a self-taught preacher, owned a circus-style tent and on weekends the family traveled throughout the region holding revivals. Mr. Johnson preached the Word while Jerry and the girls provided the music. It was here in 1949 that Jerry wrote his first gospel song, "I Can See God's Moving Hand." In 1950 Jerry and Lougenia moved to South Carolina, where he worked as a rodman during construction of the Savannah River power plant. Within two years, the marriage had begun to strain. Demanding her daughter's participation in her ministry, Lougenia's mother pressured her into joining her on the revival circuit. Jerry was happy in his job at the power plant and refused to leave. But his mother-in-law was determined to pull Lougenia away, so she went to the company and told them Jerry had lied about his age.

"I had a good job, a new car, and I was just a kid," Jerry recalls. "She turned me in—she told them how old I was. It was a government job and I had told a story on my age to get to work there. I was seventeen and I had to be twenty-one, so they terminated me. I was so upset by that, I give up my religion. That's what I done. I turned away from God. [Lougenia] went back to Florida, so I went and got her and we went to Mobile. The marriage was really over then."[2]

In 1953 Lougenia met a soldier in Mobile and, unknown to Jerry, had an affair. Jerry returned home from work one evening and found Lougenia and their children, five-year-old Gerrol, Jr. and eight-month-old Janet Rose, gone. His wife left no note and told no one of her plans to move with her paramour to his duty station in Germany. About six months later, Jerry received notice Lougenia had filed for divorce. It would be twenty-five years before Jerry was reunited with his children, who lived in Gulfport, Mississippi.

"I carried a lot of bitterness inside me over that," Jerry says. "I guess I was too young for her. And my marriage just wasn't gonna work. It was a very difficult time for me. I quit goin' to church and started makin' the clubs, drinking alcohol, fightin'. I worked the bars. I used the talent God had given me playin' in clubs.

"I don't know how I dealt with it," he says, his voice quivering at the memory of the pain. "I almost went nuts. That's the reason I have compassion on people when I see 'em do crazy things. You never know when you're talkin' to a person how bad they're hurting."[3]

Stung by humiliation and seething at betrayal, Jerry grabbed his suitcase and guitar, walked to the highway, and hitchhiked to Dayton, Ohio. In 1953 Dayton was a sleepy Midwestern town, famous as the site of the bicycle shop where Eugene and Orville Wright had designed and built the airplane they flew into the pages of history at Kitty Hawk, North Carolina, in 1903. The city was also home to

Wright Patterson Air Force Base and the National Cash Register Company. These and other industries provided employment for southern émigrés who sought alternatives to hardscrabble lives of farming or dangerous labor in coal mines.

Spirited and southern, bluegrass music was stirring the passions of young musicians who listened to Bill Monroe and His Blue Grass Boys, Flatt and Scruggs, the Stanley Brothers, and others on *Grand Ole Opry* radio broadcasts or on regional stations such as WWVA-Wheeling, West Virginia, and *Farm and Fun Time* over Bristol, Tennessee's WCYB. Bluegrass music emerged from the vision of Bill Monroe, the youngest of three brothers from Rosine, Kentucky. Monroe built bluegrass upon a foundation of Southern balladry and string band music, and added elements of the blues and jazz, along with Anglo- and African American gospel styles. His visionary blend of prewar music with innovative lyrics and driving rhythms celebrated tradition even as it nourished the progressive yearnings of music fans in the postwar South. As Monroe explained to me in 1988, "I had the blues, you know. I knew how to do it. And some Scotch [*sic*] bagpipes—that sound, the fiddle from Scotland. I put the drive in it and put the music the way I thought it should be— the high lonesome sound. And it's got a lot of gospel singing in it."[4]

Country music historian Bill C. Malone has discussed the importance of religious music in shaping the musical history of the South. "Country music has been subjected to no greater influence than religious life, which affected both the nature of songs and the manner in which they were performed. Rural southerners generally learned to sing in church, or in a milieu that stressed religious music, and they absorbed the values in the same settings that colored the lyrics and the performance of even the secular songs they sang."[5]

The role of gospel in bluegrass music is stressed by bluegrass historian Neil Rosenberg: "Religious music is found in the repertoires of most country music performers, but it has unusual prominence in the bluegrass repertoire. Religious songs constituted, on average, 30 percent of the recorded and published (in songbooks) output of the most influential early bluegrass bands—Monroe, Flatt and Scruggs, the Stanley Brothers, and Reno and Smiley."[6]

Monroe, too, was influenced by styles of music and worship he witnessed at churches in Rosine. "The first singing I ever tried to do, we'd go to church there in Rosine, Kentucky, at the Methodist or Baptist or then there was a Holiness church moved in later on. That played a part in the kind of sound and feeling I wanted to put in my music. Taken right from the gospel sound."[7]

The spirit-filled emotion that rang through the evangelical churches became an integral part of Monroe's bluegrass: "Some people, you know, don't believe in shouting in church or anything like that. Well, I have always loved to hear people shout. Anybody that can . . . I think that they should and I think they're doing wrong by holding back. . . . [T]here's holiness singing in my music, bluegrass music."[8]

Beginning in 1938, Monroe experimented with his music, searching for the right combination of sound and feeling. Then, in 1945 it came together when banjoist Earl Scruggs and guitarist/vocalist Lester Flatt joined mandolinist Monroe, fiddler Chubby Wise, and bassist Howard Watts. Monroe named the band Bill Monroe and His Blue Grass Boys in honor of his home state, Kentucky, "The Blue Grass State." With its lively tempos and instrumental brilliance, bluegrass mirrored the optimism and joy of a nation emerging victorious from sixteen years of Depression and war. By the late 1940s and early 1950s, musicians and bands began to emulate what they heard on Monroe's radio broadcasts and recordings, and bluegrass emerged as a genre, spreading far from the Kentucky and Appalachian cradle of its birth.

Although it was difficult for professional groups to earn a living, the 1950s witnessed a proliferation of regional bluegrass bands, many in Northern cities as Southerners carried their instruments and songs with them on their migration north in search of jobs. In postwar America, Dayton was a destination city for Southerners eager for work that was safer and more financially secure than the farms or coal mines they'd left behind. The emergence of Dayton as a bluegrass mecca is discussed in the wide-ranging volume *Industrial Strength Bluegrass: Southwestern Ohio's Musical Legacy*.[9]

Uprooted from nurturing families and friends, displaced Southerners sought others who spoke with the familiar patois and shared with them a common cultural heritage. Neighborhood bars provided sanctuaries from the numbing routine of assembly lines and a place to counter their alienation. These were the realities captured by country music singer Bobby Bare when he sang, "By day I make the cars / At night I make the bars," in his 1962 Grammy-winning song "Detroit City."

This is the kind of community Jerry Sullivan discovered when his last ride dropped him off in front of Mickey's bar on Dayton's 3rd Street. "I got out at Mickey's, walked in with my guitar strapped on my back, and I was met by a midget," Jerry recalls. "He said, 'Can you play that thing?' I said, 'Yes, sir.' So I took it off and I got up on that little stage and started playin' for him. When I started playin' he stopped what he was doin' and walked over to the stage. He said, 'Wait a minute. Have a drink with me. I want to call somebody.'

"So he called Red Spurlock and Red come over and listened to me. Red was the bandleader there at the time, so he hired me to play guitar and sing. They had a bluegrass band. I sang Joe Turner blues, and they wanted me to sing that so they would be a little bit different. I had to learn to play bluegrass, so Red and them would show me the difference between what I was playin' and what they played. I learned it to a fashion, got where I could play rhythm guitar, but they ended up putting me on the bass. I learned how to play some guitar there, and that was the very beginnings of my acquaintance with bluegrass music.

"The first night I played, the two midgets who owned the club get on stage and they play the upright bass fiddle. They stood an upright bass up and one got in a chair and fretted it. The other one stood on the floor and plucked the strings. They had it together, perfectly coordinated. They would get about halfway through one

Jerry Sullivan and Red Spurlock, Wiggins, Mississippi, June 3, 2005. Photograph by Jack Bernhardt.

of those fast breakdown songs and the one at the top would take his hat off and go to whuppin' the one on the floor. It would make him go faster!" Jerry lets go a belly laugh as memory of the circus-like scene flits into view.

It didn't take long for his bluegrass pals to recognize Jerry's talent and his engaging personality. In the clubs, his circle of friends grew larger and he added bluegrass to his repertoire of gospel, rhythm and blues, and blues. "They called the place Mickey's for a long time, then they named it the Station Inn. That's where Jimmy Martin, Sonny Osborne and a lot of people played. Across the street was the Spur. That's where Red Allen, Noah Crase, Johnny McKee and Frank Wakefield played before he joined with us. I could hear them sing that harmony and it was real pretty. I met Sonny Osborne there because he was workin' with Jimmy Martin. Sonny was very young and boy, he could play so well.

"I hung around . . . with Red Spurlock and found anybody who would pick with me. The Station Inn furnished me an apartment, plus Red paid us $20 a night to pick. I had a free place to live. That seemed like big money—we thought we was big time. The Station Inn was just packed. People would shuttle in and out. They'd sit and listen to us awhile, then go listen to Red [Allen] awhile. That was a big thing. That's how I learned about the music I wanted to play. I was playing Joe Turner blues at that time. And I'd played gospel. I begin to hear something in bluegrass music when I first heard it in Dayton.

"Then we all come down South—Red Allen, Johnny McKee, Frank Wakefield, Red Spurlock, myself. We played in Mobile at radio stations and were the first people to take bluegrass into the clubs down here."[10]

When his bandmates returned to Ohio, Jerry remained in Alabama longing to be near his family and haunted by the loss of his children. Needing work, Jerry and his brother Aubrey lit out for Birmingham. One evening after work, Jerry was drawn to the lively sounds of a boogie-woogie piano tune coming from one of Birmingham's bars. He walked in and saw a short, slightly built man pounding out rhythm and blues with the emotional fervor of a Joe Turner or a Jimmy Reed. "I listened to that little dude play a little bit, and I said, 'He is fantastic,'" Jerry recalls of Dean Mathis, the piano player he would soon christen "Pee Wee" in deference to his short stature.

A few years younger than Jerry, Louis Aldine "Dean" Mathis had left home in Bremen, Georgia, and joined Paul Howard's fabled Arkansas Cotton Pickers, a western swing outfit that performed regularly over 50,000-watt, clear channel station KWKH in Shreveport, Louisiana. The centerpiece of the station's programming was the *Louisiana Hayride*, a country music variety show similar to Nashville's *Grand Ole Opry*. Originating from Shreveport's Municipal Auditorium, the program featured some of the era's most prominent country and rockabilly acts. Elvis performed on the Hayride early in his career, as did Hank Williams, Webb Pierce, Kitty Wells, and Johnny Cash. In the 1960s, Dean, his brother Mark, along with high-pitched falsetto singer Larry Henley formed the

Newbeats, a pop/rock trio best remembered for their 1964 million-selling hit, "Bread and Butter."[11]

But in the 1950s, Mathis was earning a living playing piano in Birmingham's bars. He was waiting for the next gig to come along, when Jerry Sullivan sauntered in and sidled up to the piano. The two musicians took an instant liking to each other, musically and personally, beginning a friendship that continues today.

"Pee Wee and I got to playin' and we got to findin' out we could do stuff with a rhythm guitar and a piano—just the two instruments. We worked up some of the finest stuff, and we'd write songs. He said, 'I worked last year with Paul Howard. Did you ever hear of him?' I said, 'Sure I've heard of Paul Howard, the 'Arkansas Cotton Picker.'' Pee Wee said, 'Well, he's doin' some shows down in Louisiana. I'll call him and see if he'll take us on.'"

Booking acts for the Hayride's package shows, Howard was searching for new talent. He invited Jerry and Dean to audition, and offered them a job opening shows for Elvis and other Hayride stars. Dean's piano riffs and Jerry's solid rhythm guitar and sonorous baritone were the perfect vehicle for rockabilly music—the revved-up, sexually charged hybrid of country music and rhythm and blues that spurred the transition from placid pop to rowdy rock and roll.

"Paul Howard took us to the Hayride," Jerry says. "That was quite an experience for us. Boy, I really liked Paul Howard. He got where he could book Pee Wee and I. We had this little act together, you know, where we could do all of these blues, and I could do my Elvis act, and all of this stuff. We could just stay workin', you know. And a lot of places, Pee Wee would go in and he'd tell 'em he had this blues act that they needed to see. Well, I'd be sittin' over in the booth. He'd say, 'Man, you ain't seen nothin' 'til you see this dude play. I'll bring him on.' He was so good on the piano, man, we could just shake the house. We'd learned all that Joe Turner stuff with all the breaks in it—real lively, you know. That was so much fun to do. That's a part of my life I really enjoyed doin' because I learned a lot about myself and a lot about music with him. I said, 'I want this to be part of what I do when I finally dig in. I don't want to forget this sound, or this beat."[12]

In 1954 the duo made a 45 rpm recording for Shreveport's Vee Records, featuring Jerry's composition "Ella Mae" along with the Callahan Brothers' 1934 hit "She's My Curly Headed Baby." Just as the act was beginning to find success, Jerry was drafted into the army. By the time he was discharged in 1957, rockabilly had morphed into full-blown rock and roll. Jerry would never record another rockabilly song, but turned, instead, to making a joyful gospel noise unto the Lord.

# Chapter 5

# A Strength by Me
## Jerry, Tammy, and New Beginnings

For traveling musicians, the road is a force of imposing contradictions. Indispensable for earning a living, the road is haunted with traffic horrors memorialized in such death-song tragedies as Roy Acuff's "Wreck on the Highway" and Randy Travis's "Three Wooden Crosses." There's more than a hint of danger in this life as logging trucks full of loads and chemical tankers pass us at full throttle, while Bob guides the bus between the white lines along two-lane rural roadways.

The Sullivans have logged hundreds of thousands of miles by car and bus, taking their ministry to churches and festivals, political rallies, and tent revivals up and down the back roads of the Deep South. For Jerry, it seems every crossroad, water tank, and levee along the way conjures memories of a memorable concert, a bus breakdown, or an impish prank pulled by Emmett Sullivan on an unsuspecting preacher or bandmate.

We're on our way to Lake Cove, Louisiana, for a concert at Brother David Messer's Happy Hollow Holiness Church, and three churches in east Texas. It's a route Sullivans have traveled since 1949. As we pass by Jackson, Mississippi, Jerry's mood turns somber. "This is where we had the crash," he says, his voice quieting to near-whisper.

Sullivan Family Gospel Singers, 1960s. L-R: Emmett Sullivan, Jerry Sullivan, Margie Sullivan, Enoch Sullivan. Photograph courtesy of Tammy Sullivan.

Around 10:30 p.m. on March 13, 1977, the Sullivan Family was returning home from a concert in Louisiana. It was a familiar, ordinary drive, similar to dozens they had made on this same route for nearly thirty years. With Margie in the passenger's seat, Enoch drove while Emmett and Jerry slept in the back seat. None was wearing a seat belt.

As the Sullivans drove east, a man returning from an automobile race at Alabama's Talladega racetrack was towing a race car in the westbound lane. Suddenly, the flat-bed trailer broke loose from his car and rocketed across the median, slamming head-on into the Sullivans' Ford station wagon.

"We never seen it," Jerry explains. "It just bounced across the road and set down in front of us. We hit it head-on. I was in the back seat.

I come up over top of Enoch and I pushed him and the steering wheel down and my head hit the rim of the sun visor. It just peeled my—it took two layers of my skull with it. Glass worked out of my head for a year after that. It broke Margie's leg, it cracked Enoch's ribs, hurt Emmett's back, and I had a head injury. That's what took me outta the Sullivan Family. I was replaced in that group."[1]

Two months after the accident, Enoch and Margie were back on the road, while Jerry sat home, recovering from his injuries. His scalp wound required seventy-five stitches, affected his memory, and resulted in periodic blackouts that kept him from performing for over two years. According to Jerry, Enoch and Margie announced they would continue without him, an unceremonious split inflicting an emotional wound from which Jerry never recovered. With the closeness of siblings, Jerry and Enoch grew up playing and singing together to accompany Brother Arthur's preaching. And Jerry had written many of the songs that were staples in the Sullivan Family repertoire, among them "I Can See God's Moving Hand," "Born Again Experience," and "Sing Daddy a Song." Now, his nephew had severed their bond, and Jerry faced a dark, uncertain future.

Jerry's recovery was physically and emotionally difficult. Unable to work, he hoped to receive some money from the one-million-dollar lawsuits filed by Enoch and Margie,[2] which would help pay for hospital bills and doctor visits. Experiencing periodic blackouts and memory loss, he lived with the twin fears that he may never fully recover from his injuries, and that he might not be able to resume life as a songwriter and performer.

Watching her father suffer was painful for Tammy. She idolized her father, and from an early age was captivated by his music and his role in the Sullivan Family Gospel Singers. Because of Jerry's blackouts, watching him try to sing in church in the two years following the accident was fraught with anxiety. "When we went to church after that wreck, we would have to watch Daddy because he would have these blackout spells," Tammy recalls. "I remember

several nights in church, he would just faint—with the guitar—
somebody would grab the guitar and set him down."³

Struggling to regain his health, Jerry sank into depression and
seemed poised to give up on music until Tammy, who had just
turned thirteen, offered encouragement: "Dad was sitting on the
couch and he said, 'I don't know what I'll do.' We was gettin' ready to
go to church, and I said, 'Don't worry about it. You can write some
more songs and I'll learn how to sing 'em and I'll help you.' That's
how we started. When she told me that, it meant everything in the
world to me," Jerry says. "She said, 'Daddy, don't you give up. I'll get
up there aside of you. I'll learn how to play *somethin'* and I'll help
ya.' In just a short time she was a *strength* by me."⁴

At first, Tammy was shy, hiding behind her father when folks
approached to compliment her and Jerry on their performance.
Inexperienced and searching for her style, Tammy wasn't sure how
to phrase or use dynamics when singing one of her father's songs.
Longtime friend Marty Stuart was a singing coach to Tammy and
an inspiration to her dad. "Marty would have to take her over in the
corner and tell her how to sing her words," Jerry says. Stuart, who
began playing mandolin at age twelve with Enoch and Margie, also
helped Jerry regain his confidence and was instrumental in helping
Jerry and Tammy initiate their ministry. "The blow on the head had
caused me to lose confidence in myself—my ability to do things,"
Jerry says. "You could hear it in my voice, and in my playin' a little
bit. But Marty would say, 'Forget that! Come on and do it!'"⁵

As he began his recovery, Jerry moved to Nashville, where he took
a job parking tractor-trailer rigs. He also returned to performing
part-time, playing bass for Bill Monroe's Blue Grass Boys and for
the Midnight Ramblers, the band headed by Monroe's son, James.
Being involved once again with music instilled in Jerry the confidence to put the Sullivan Family behind him and start fresh with
his daughter at his side.

Jerry and Tammy Sullivan released their first album in 1979.
Titled *Country Voice Records Present Jerry and Tammy Sullivan*,

the twelve-song cassette boasts a Who's Who of bluegrass musicians, including Blaine Sprouse (fiddle), Alan O'Bryant (banjo), and Joe Stuart (guitar, mandolin, and bass); Marty Stuart played guitar, mandolin, and fiddle. The album features songs penned by Jerry, several of which he had performed with Enoch and Margie, and which remain staples of the Jerry and Tammy repertoire: "God's Mighty Power," "From the Manger to the Garden," "Memories of Daddy," and other originals share billing with "Morning Train," "Old Rugged Cross," and other gospel favorites.[6]

With the album in hand, Jerry and Tammy began making phone calls to preachers who might book them at churches where Jerry had performed with the Sullivan Family. Perhaps out of deference to Enoch and Margie, or possibly because they were unwilling to take a chance on a new act, all but one declined. It appeared the duo's career would stumble out of the gate until the Rev. David Messer, a self-taught Holiness preacher and sawmill operator from remote Lake Cove, Louisiana, invited Jerry and Tammy to begin their ministry with a singing at his Happy Hollow Holiness Church.

April 23, we leave Mississippi and drive west through Ferriday, Louisiana. The bus carries Jerry and Jerry's younger daughter, Stephanie, JP Cormier, and me. Ferriday is home to rock and roll wild man Jerry Lee Lewis, and his famous cousins, country singer and nightclub owner Mickey Gilley and the tarnished televangelist, Jimmy Swaggart. Brother Swaggart, star of his own evangelical television show was recently embroiled in scandal, arrested in his car with a female prostitute. As we enter the city limits, we're greeted by a familiar regiment of signs announcing the Kiwanis Club, Rotary Club, and other organizations of Ferriday's civic pride. Jerry is disappointed that a sign proclaiming Ferriday as home of the famous trio has been removed. "I guess Swag swung too swanky for 'em," he quips, referring to the Reverend's scandal. "They don't love him anymore."[7]

East Louisiana is poor, flat farmland. Its dull, shapeless plain finds relief only from the long linear levee rising from the valley floor to protect homes and farmland from the Mississippi River's threatening floods. It may have seemed "a treat to beat your feet on the Mississippi mud," as sung by Bing Crosby, Dinah Shore, Bobby Darin, and other entertainers who may have never lived through a devastating flood. But the song, "Mississippi Mud," was less celebratory to those who survived in 1927 when the Mississippi poured over its banks and flooded 23,000 square miles of land covering seven states. This was seventy-eight years before Hurricane Katrina in 2005, when two hundred forty-six people were killed and 700,000 displaced from their homes.[8]

Blackwater swamps and drainage ditches line the winding two-lane highway; signs point the way to Workinger's Bayou and advertise nylon fishing nets manufactured in nearby Jonesville. We watch men dip nets into a drainage ditch and scoop crawfish into plastic pails. We pass Mt. Beulah Christian Church and other aging grey temples, all traces of paint erased by decades of wind and rain.

West of Jonesville, Jerry stops the bus and welcomes aboard his old friend Dean Mathis, who will accompany us to Happy Hollow Holiness Church. Mathis is a multi-instrumentalist and lifelong professional musician. In 1964 his band, the Newbeats, had a #2 hit with their million-selling novelty song, "Bread and Butter." He and Jerry had worked together as a rockabilly duo in Birmingham and later with country star Paul Howard on Shreveport's *Louisiana Hayride*.

Jerry and Pee Wee have seen each other occasionally through the years, and Pee Wee has attended Homecoming at Victory Grove Church. But Jerry is especially excited about this reunion because he has brought with him a copy of the rare 45 rpm record he and Pee Wee made together in 1955. Their recording of Jerry's "Ella Mae" helped them land their gig with Howard.

With Pee Wee aboard, the road's relentless monotony is relieved as we listen to the old friends reminisce about their time with Howard, playing the Hayride, and opening for Elvis. They laugh about the night in Little Rock, Arkansas, when a group of teenage girls gathered around a glistening white Cadillac parked behind the theater. With red lipstick, the girls wrote I LOVE YOU ELVIS and other messages on the car. Jerry and Pee Wee chortle as they tell how Howard emerged from the evening to find the Elvis tribute and other messages in flaming red lipstick scrawled across his brand-new white Caddy.

Pee Wee started playing professionally at age seventeen with Harold Shedd, future president of PolyGram Records and a legendary Nashville record producer. Pee Wee says he was hired to play fiddle for country star Faron Young, even though he knew how to play only two tunes on the devil's box. And that before he formed the Newbeats, he and a friend had a recording contract with the legendary rhythm and blues label Chess.

Jerry turns off the paved road leading to Turkey Creek, and begins to steer the bus carefully along dirt and gravel roads surrounded by pine and hardwood forests. Driving deep into the woods, Jerry turns to me and says, "Brother David don't have to worry about the IRS findin' him. The government don't even know he exists."[9]

Spanish moss dangles from trees like fuzzy brown tinsel as we cross Turkey Creek and pass a muddy brown gravel pit pond on the right. Jokingly, Stephanie says this is the community swimming hole, even though an ominous handwritten sign warns: "CLOSE [sic] DUE TO DEQ REGULATIONS."

Logging roads lead from the dirt drive and disappear into the woods; we spy two Cajuns sipping beer at a table outside the Hornet's Nest bar. Another handwritten sign, tacked askew to a pine tree, announces "BubbA's Place 1 MILE" offering a source of rest and relaxation for loggers at the end of long, hard days on the saw.

Jerry maneuvers the bus around the narrow turns of Lake Cove, past white trailer homes with satellite dishes beaming the outside world to this community of Cajun foresters. Jerry parks the bus atop a hill looking down upon a rustic frame building nestled among trees on the valley floor below. This is Happy Hollow

Happy Hollow Holiness Church, Lake Cove, Louisiana, April 1993. Photograph by Jack Bernhardt.

Holiness, the church Brother David built from logs he sawed in the sawmill he built from scratch behind the church. Born and raised in Lake Cove, Brother David is a lifelong woodsman and jack-of-all-trades. Independence and self-sufficiency are theological and practical imperatives for David and his wife, Sister Trisha. David delivered all seven of his children in their home, and the children are home-schooled by Trisha. The oldest boy, Jason, works in the woods beside his father.

Happy Hollow Holiness Church is a simple, wood-frame structure cobbled together from scavenged and donated materials as well as lumber cut from the surrounding woods. The sanctuary is small, its blue wooden pews seating perhaps fifty worshippers. The wall behind the altar is adorned with a full-sized wallpaper mural depicting a dense forest of red- and gold-leafed trees. It's as if Brother David has erected a shrine to the patron saint of loggers, offering thanks for providing employment and identity for the generations of woodsmen who have lived and toiled within.

A rectangular, tin-roofed fellowship hall, no longer in use, extends thirty feet from the right side of the church. On the left, a sheltered walkway leads from the sanctuary to restrooms which dump their untreated wastes into a small branch running behind the church. This disregard for sanitation prompted the Louisiana Department of Environmental Quality to close the pit pond, and has forced some but not all Lake Cove residents to rely on bottled water for cooking and drinking.

One of ten children, Brother David was born with a congenital speech defect. He speaks and preaches with distortions heard in the speech pattern of others in this genetically close community. While difficult at first for a newcomer to understand, Brother David's congregation doesn't seem to notice when he orates passionately about the goodness of the Lord, or sings the old gospel hymns while banging out chords on his guitar. Muscular and fit at forty years old, Brother David has followed his father into the woods, while finding his vocation as a man of the Lord. David and his wife, Sister Trisha, live in a house they built above the church. Brother David has followed the Sullivan Family since the 1950s. He was first to book Jerry and Tammy when they began their ministry in 1979. "I like the music they were playin', and I like the spirit they have. They are loving people. I love music and I love bluegrass music, so that really set me on fire.

"I was born and raised in Lake Cove, and my father and them lived here about seventy years," Brother David says. "My mother originally came from a little place out of Rapides Parish. My father and mother met, then they got married. My father's family lived there probably 150–200 years back. His dad died when he was nine years old, so my dad had to go out and make a livin' workin' in a sawmill. From that, he kept on workin' way on up 'til he got old enough to work on the cross-cut saw. Him and his brother were real popular. Everyone in the area talked about them on the cross-cut saw, because no one could keep up with them 'cause they were so good.

"I started preaching in a little church called Living Waters Tabernacle when I was about nineteen years old. My dad wasn't no preacher, but he was a real good Christian; my mama was, too. My dad backed the church real hard. He supplied most of the money wherever he went. And the labor, too. If anything needed to be done, they always looked to my dad to do it. Even back before we went to Living Water Tabernacle Church, we had a little church in Lake

Brother David and Sister Trisha Messer, Happy Hollow Holiness Church, March 2023. Photo by Jack Bernhardt.

Cove, a half mile from where Happy Hollow Church is. My dad was one of the deacons in that church—old-time holiness.

"We go by 'independent holiness'—we don't attach no name to it. We went to that church for years, and finally it burned down. During the week, my mother picked cotton. So we'd all go out to the cotton field and pick. When potato season came in, we dug sweet potatoes. My whole family worked. My dad worked in the sawmill, and we worked in the fields picking cotton and taters. After I got to be about sixteen years old, I started to work in the woods with my dad, haulin' pulp wood and saw logs."

Brother David pauses and reflects on his family and the power of prayer. "We had ten children in our family, five boys and five girls. One brother died when he was a baby. My mama and sister and niece got killed in an automobile wreck by an alcoholic. My dad was in critical condition; he lived five years but he never walked. He died three times in ICU. But through prayers, the Lord miraculously brought him back from the dead. Finally, I asked the Lord to take him home, and the Lord answered my prayers."[10]

The concert is scheduled to begin at 7:00 p.m. But by mid-afternoon, changes in the program are underway. The church's piano is badly out of tune, and Stephanie did not bring her portable keyboard on this trip. This means that Stephanie will not be part of tonight's performance. Also, sore throats that have bothered the Sullivans since leaving Wagarville have worsened, leaving them weak and in poor voice. Still, the show must go on.

At the microphone, Jerry Sullivan is an imposing figure, his rough-hewn working-class frame clothed in the garb of civility. Fifty-nine years old and five feet nine inches tall, Jerry carries most of his 240 pounds above and over his belt, a wide black leather strap that wraps round his waist, binding the loose drape of his black polyester pants to the pressed tidiness of his white dress shirt. The conservative cut of his clothes is accented by a flame-red necktie with white cross emblem hanging loosely from his collar, unbuttoned for comfort and a hint of casualness in the formal sanctity of the church. Lights beam down from overhead, and Jerry's glossy black patent leather cowboy boots with silver toe guards glisten from beneath his pants cuffs. Flashes of light from his Martin D-28 guitar's spruce top dance random patterns on the walls as he sways to the rhythms Tammy thumps out on the upright bass. I recognize this costume as the same style of stage outfit Jerry, Enoch, and Emmett wear in a 1960s publicity photo hanging on the wall of the Sullivans' office in Wagarville.

Performing as a trio, Jerry, Tammy, and John Paul kick off the concert with a snappy version of "I Can See God's Moving Hand." There are fifty-two persons in attendance, including the eight members of Brother David's immediate family. From the stage, the Sullivans recognize the Causey family. J.A. and Genevie Causey parented twelve children, including Jonathan who, as a teen, spent a summer living with Jerry and Zelma in Wagarville. Jonathan was an aspiring musician who lived with his hosts until moving back home, graduating high school, and starting a bluegrass gospel ministry of his own. Years later, Jonathan would become Tammy's third husband.

Singers with such bayou names as Obeira and Bessie Gayle made a joyful noise singing "I Saw Mother in a Vison" and Jerry Sullivan's "If You Want to Go Up," which Bessie Gayle renamed "The TV Preacher." Brother David and family also take the stage to sing Jason's "I Just Touched Jesus" and Jerry's "Devil's Level." While all but the Sullivans are amateur singers, they sing in voices passionate as they are infused with a thick bayou brogue. This is a part of the South that retains its identity long after it's been diluted in the urban centers of Atlanta, Birmingham, and other metropolitan areas. Tonight's audience provides a meager $110 offering to the Sullivans for this gospel sing.

Friday morning, Jerry pulls the bus out of Lake Cove, and steers toward Livingston, Texas. Sore throats have worsened for Jerry, Tammy, Stephanie, and JP, whose throats are swollen and red. The family worries they won't be able to meet their weekend obligations. But, like entertainers in other genres, the Sullivans do not wish to disappoint their fans. Ill or injured, traveling evangelists are vulnerable as they toil away from the comfort and care of family, friends, and home.

We spend the night as guests of Margie Sullivan's cousin, Sylvia, where we have breakfast and shower before heading west to Texas. A headline in the morning paper trumpets the conviction of Alabama governor Guy Hunt, who was found guilty of misappropriation of government funds totaling $200,000 which he used to purchase marble showers and other charges. Five days earlier, Federal agents had surrounded the Branch Davidian compound in Waco, Texas, and attempted to arrest David Koresh, the sect's charismatic leader. A gunfight erupted and the compound was set ablaze, killing some 120 residents. Jerry Sullivan believes these transgressions derive from "Satan turning Christians against each other, and men putting themselves above other men." All this, Jerry says, is the fulfillment of Biblical prophecy hastening Christ's Second Coming.

— ☦ —

It's half-past five when Jerry pulls the bus into the empty parking lot of Livingston's Oakdale Baptist Church. Oakdale Baptist is a wood-frame church with rusting metal roof, converted years ago from a one-room schoolhouse. Inside, the floor is covered in bright red carpet with matching red-cushions on pine wood pews. A mural depicting a river—the Jordan River, perhaps?—adorns the rear wall of the altar. A fiberglass robin's-egg blue baptismal tub sits in front of the mural. A sheet of clear plexiglass stretches across the bottom protecting the altar's carpet from damage during water-immersed baptisms. A bulletin board at altar's front reads:

| | |
|---|---|
| Enrollment | 40 |
| Offering Today | 235.00 |
| Offering Last Sunday | 486.25 |
| Attendance Today | 27 |
| Attendance Last Sunday | 77 |
| Sunday School | 14 |

Two hymn books are in the pews. *Heavenly Highway Hymns*, compiled by Luther G. Presley and dated 1956, is shape-note only. The second is written in standard music notation.

Forty patrons attend the evening's singing. The Sullivans perform without complaint or mention of their illness, and the audience seems to enjoy the music. Jerry's family friend, Regina, is at tonight's concert, and joins the Sullivans to sing "Tell Me Again There Is No God," a contemporary gospel song written by Walter Bailes of West Virginia's famed Bailes Brothers. Afterwards, Regina tells Jerry about Livingston Medical Clinic, and suggests they stop by the clinic in the morning.[11]

Tonight, we sleep on the bus. The bunk beds with cushy mattresses offer luxury accommodations compared with the cramped automobiles that quartered earlier generations of traveling minstrels. In the morning, Jerry and Tammy complain of worsening soreness in their throats. Jerry and Stephanie have no health insurance, but Tammy is covered under Aubrey's work policy. I offer to pay for

Jerry, Stephanie, and John Paul. Jerry declines until I ask him to accept my offer as a gift to his ministry.

We arrive at Livingston Clinic at 10:45. The clinic charges a "new patient fee." So rather than $25 for an office visit, each patient will be charged "$37, which is less expensive than the $55 fee charged by the emergency room across the street." The clinic physician offers a "package deal," charging one new and one established patient $62 for treatment.

Waiting in the lobby, I survey the literature on tables and book shelves, and leaf through *The Evangelist: The Voice of the Jimmy Swaggart Ministries*. A variety of other magazines, books, and fliers makes clear this clinic identifies as a Christian facility, though it does not cater to Christians exclusively. Soon, the Sullivans appear in the lobby, their systems treated with antibiotics. The attending physician tells me he's a fan of the Sullivans' music and faith, and charges a discounted fee. This evangelical subculture nurtures itself.[12]

Our next stop is Shepherd, San Jacinto County, Texas, where the band will play a benefit for the Shepherd Volunteer Fire Department. The show features several groups performing at the Shepherd High School. We discover the benefit is happening at the same time as the school's prom, which reduces the number of parents and students who might attend the benefit. The audience numbers seventy-eight mostly senior citizens on break from the nursing home behind the firehouse. Grizzled ranch hands are easily identified by their straw or beaver fur cowboy hats, and mud caked against the cuffs of their jeans. San Jacinto is a poor county, and the benefit earned less money than Jerry had hoped. He is subdued as he guides the bus down the road toward Leggett Assembly of God Church in Leggett, Texas.

It's 10:30 a.m. as Jerry parks the bus in the parking lot of Leggett Assembly of God church. Founded in 1914, Assemblies of God is the world's largest Pentecostal denomination, with some 13,000

churches in the United States alone. Televangelist Jimmy Swaggart's ministry is a member. It may be no coincidence that we are greeted in the parking lot by a young, impeccably groomed man in his late twenties. With his round face, dark suit and tie, hair slicked back and coifed to perfection, the young man appears to be Reverend Swaggart's doppelganger. He leads us into the church, where Jerry, Tammy, and Aubrey slide into the first pew. Jerry nods in agreement as the lady evangelist expounds on chapter-and-verse of the Bible.

The evangelist has prepared her sermon, but lacks the fire and inspiration one might expect from a Pentecostal preacher. This may explain why only fourteen celebrants attend. As the service draws to a close, the audience swells to seventy-seven in anticipation of music featuring the Sullivans. The audience arrives in a variety of new and older model cars and pickup trucks. A rusting Ford Fairmont sports bumper stickers that read: I THE BIBLE (The heart no longer visible) and AMERICAN ABORTION HITLER WOULD HAVE LOVED IT [swastikas at each end).

A Brown Ford van displays a bumper sticker referencing President Bill Clinton and his wife, Hillary: IMPEACH THE PRESIDENT! AND GET RID OF HER HUSBAND TOO!!!

A Chevrolet minivan advertises 89.3 FM KSBJ CHRISTIAN MUSIC GOD LISTENS. One gentleman says he owns a body shop; business is slow, he offers, because "everyone's holding on to their money and not getting their fenders fixed." I suggest perhaps people are driving more carefully. He's not amused.

The church's attendance and offering board reads; Attendance goal, 150. Attendance last Sunday, 49. Offering last Sunday, 26.81. Attendance today, 41. Offering today, 33.82. Number on the roll, 62. Average attendance, 76.[13]

We leave Leggett and head toward Point Blank, where the Sullivans will do their last gig before the long drive to Wagarville. Jerry says that despite the lean offerings, the Leggett pastor wrote him a check for $500, which will turn the corner on meeting expenses. The pastor was pleased with the singing, and wants to bring the band back for a large event with combined churches. Spirits are high as we drive toward Point Blank. Ailments are under control, and Jerry says the income from Leggett "made the weekend." He calls it a "gift from God."

Seventy-five persons attend the singing at Point Blank's First Baptist Church. The pastor, Rev. Wilburn Ansley, says the Point Blank area consists of retired senior citizens, along with schoolteachers and other professionals. "There's just not really a lot of work here; they have to drive into Houston, or Huntsville, or Livingstone or some other town. Because sawmills, public schools—that's about all there is unless they drive a long distance to go to work. There's sawmills all through these woods."[14] Seventy-four churches are listed in the phone book of the Eastex Telephone Cooperative, whose motto is "A phone for every farm." Thirty-seven, or 50 percent, of the churches are Baptist.

Rev. Ansley had booked the Sullivans in years past, and is grateful they are willing to perform for his congregation. "A lot of groups won't come to a small town," he says. "But a small church needs to be ministered to just as much as the larger churches. I thank God for the Sullivans, because they'll come by faith to sing. Of course, I plead for our people to give all they can, and I praise God they'll do that, but they're very limited in their ability to give. The Sullivans help me in my ministry in the sense that they are always a blessing to the church."[15]

The Point Blank congregation yielded a $300 "love offering." Rev. Ansley told Jerry he would like to book the band at some future date. "We know this," Jerry says of their reception as we leave the church, "the back roads is very much alive to us."[16]

At 8:30 p.m., we begin the 550-mile, fifteen-hour journey home to Wagarville. Some of us will sleep through the night. Jerry and Bob will pull off the road and grab a few hours of sleep before continuing on to Alabama, Zelma, and the comfort of their own beds.

*Chapter 6*

# Tammy Sullivan
*Praise the Lord for This Life I'm Living*

Life hasn't always been easy for Tammy Sullivan. For every triumph, it seems God has tested her with challenges that would wither the faith of a woman of lesser resolve. But through them all—financial worries, family concerns, hardships of life on the road—Tammy has never wavered from her commitment to singing the gospel songs written by her father. Honoring Tammy for her ardor, Jerry and Marty Stuart composed "Praise the Lord for This Life I'm Living," which appears on Jerry and Tammy's *Tomorrow* CD, released on Ricky Skaggs' Ceili Records label in 2000:

> The world can turn in all its glory
> But I was born to tell the story
> Of the one that broke the chains that fastened me
> To a world that was never lasting
>
> In my heart a fire is burning
> For the one who's soon returning
> Then He'll have full attention
> And I shall have blessed redemption

Chorus:
I'm free, I'm saved from sin and sorrow
Come what may be, there no tomorrow
All my heart and soul I'm giving
Praise the Lord, Praise the Lord for this life I'm living

The night is dark, the way is lonely
God loves me like His one and only
He knows my heart and my intentions
And every chance His name I'll mention

Grief and sorrow, I'm not keeping, friend
This is not the time for weeping
I stand on faith proclaiming power
While drawing closer is the hour

"This song brings it all together for me," Tammy says. "And I do praise Him just like the opening line says: 'The world can turn in all its glory / but I was born to tell the story.' I truly do believe that. I've come to realize that's what I'm here for. I *was* born to tell the Gospel story. I'm just praisin' the Lord now for the life I'm livin'. I'm so happy where I am. Everything I've been through, I don't regret it. I'm excited about it, and I know it's put me where I am."[1]

Tammy has never known a time when her father didn't play music. At home, in church, and at festivals, or when visiting cousins Enoch and Margie in neighboring St. Stephens, music was always at the center of family life. Whenever possible, she accompanied her father to Sullivan Family gigs, but most of the time she waited with Zelma for her dad to return from his travels.

"When they were leavin' out on trips, I always wanted to go," Tammy recalls. "He would let me go to different places like bluegrass concerts and gospel singin's. When I didn't get to go, we would see him on television. The Sullivan Family had a TV program every Sunday. I remember Mama tellin' me, 'Well you can't go, but we'll watch him

Tammy Sullivan on bass. Photograph by Jack Bernhardt.

on TV. But I always wanted to go with him. And when I *did* get to go, there was somethin' about it that it always touched me. I'd say, 'That's what I want to do, to get up there just like Daddy and help him.'"

As a senior in the Leroy High School class of 1982, Tammy realized her dreams were different from those of her classmates. She didn't date, she went to gospel singings. On Sundays and Wednesdays, she accompanied her family at church. For most teenagers in and around Wagarville, life after graduation meant getting a job in one of south Alabama's chemical plants or with the Walmart Superstore in nearby Jackson. But Tammy dreamt of standing on stage with her father and singing, the way Margie sang beside Enoch.

"Music was always there," she remembers. "When Daddy was home, he would write songs. He would stay in his room, and he'd say, 'Y'all be real quiet,'cause I gotta try to do this tape.' He would be writin' songs. I remember him writin' 'He Lives' in the bedroom. He's goin', 'I gotta get this right.' And I'd laugh and say, 'But Daddy, I want you to come out.' He'd say, 'Just one more minute.' And he was writin' that beautiful song. It was quite different from everybody else I went to school with. They didn't understand why I wanted to do what I wanted to do. They'd say, 'You need to get a job at the chemical plant. That's what everybody around here does.' Not me! I always wanted to sing with my Daddy, and I'm just glad I've got the opportunity to do it."[2]

For two years after the car crash, Tammy watched her father struggle with memory and self-confidence. Enoch and Margie had resumed their career without Jerry, who sank deeper into depression and self-doubt. Tammy never lost faith in her father, and promised to help him find his way back to health and his music.

The father-daughter team released their first album, *Country Voice Records Present Jerry and Tammy Sullivan*, in 1979.[3] While Jerry's soothing, resonant baritone carries his familiar warmth, his singing is restrained, as if to avoid overwhelming Tammy's youthful, tentative efforts. Tammy's singing on this tape echoes Margie's old-time country voicing, a style similar to country vocalists Molly O'Day and Wilma Lee Cooper. Tammy idolized and modeled herself after Margie, her larger-than-life cousin who was regarded as gospel music royalty as well as family.

"I was surrounded by my family's singing, and Margie was the only lady singer that I heard for a long time growing up," Tammy says. "I loved her singing. I didn't have a lot of formal teaching. All I had to go by was what my dad tried to show me. And him being a male voice, it was hard for him to show me exactly the way I could understand it. I tried to translate what he was sayin'. Then I heard Margie, and loved what she did."

While Margie was inspired by the old-time singing of the Carter Family and Molly O'Day, Tammy's influences also included the emotional delivery of country music star Connie Smith and the religious fervor of Dorothy Love Coates, the African American gospel great and fellow Alabamian. "I love the rhythm in Dorothy Love's voice," Tammy says. "The rhythm and the soul and the feelin'. She's happy, and she preaches it. It's like rock and roll. I love the raw edge in her voice because it's not so perfect."[4]

Tammy also learned phrasing from male singers, especially from the Nashville Bluegrass Band's Alan O'Bryant, who played with Jerry as a member of James Monroe's Midnight Ramblers, and the late fiddler and Blue Grass Boy alumnus Joe Stuart, who performed and recorded with the Sullivans through the years.

"Alan is one of my favorite singers," Tammy says. "A lot of his turns, I got to hear 'em firsthand. They'd have little jam sessions and he'd sing all night or come to our house and sing all day. I got to actually *see* him do it and hear him do it. It made a big difference when I could actually see somebody do it. Daddy would show me how to sing, but he didn't have a lot of the turns that I was wantin' to do. So when I actually saw and heard Alan, that's when I started developin' a lot of my turns.

"And Joe Stuart. As far as the bluesy, soul-type of singin', I got to see and hear him firsthand. Somethin' else I got from him—when I was learnin' to sing 'Working on a Building,' I would sing the lead with him. He had a weird way of sayin' 'I' m workin' on a building.' It was sort of how he played the fiddle—snatchy-like. I liked the rhythm of the way he said it. So I learned that from him, that little shuffle in the chorus."

While Tammy listened to a variety of female vocalists, she took her father's advice and worked toward developing her own distinctive sound. "My dad always told me, 'It's good to be influenced by people, but the thing you want to remember is to do it in your own style, do it the way you can and from what you feel inside your heart. And when it's all said and done, it will be you and people will recognize your voice.'"[5] Thus, Tammy adorns her songs with subtle, ornamental flourishes that transform them from routine presentations to personalized works of vocal art.

Tammy's robust, textured vocal style, heard on songs such as "I Can See God's Moving Hand" and the a cappella spiritual medley, "Up Above My Head/Blind Bartimus," seems to embody the Pentecostal fire that ignites the family's spiritual quest. As Tammy explains, her music is an expression of the strength of her faith: "What I love in a female singer is *power*. I don't like as much a laid-back, softer voice. I like the powerful voice that gets the message out. The type of church I've been in all my life is Pentecostal. And the message, when the preacher preaches, is a driving, shouting delivery—fiery. When I go to sing, I think of that and say, well, I like that delivery that I hear from the pulpit. If I can deliver my song like that, that's the way I want it delivered and projected to the audience—with *fire* in it."[6]

It may have been the fire in Tammy's singing that caught the ear of Tony Brown, head of Nashville's MCA Records. A former keyboard player for Elvis Presley and Emmylou Harris, Brown is among the most respected men in the country music industry. He offered to assist Tammy in pursuing a country music recording contract. Tammy declined, telling Brown her life's work was singing her father's songs.

"I never had a desire to become a famous gospel star or country music singer," Tammy says. "For me, it's all about the love of the music and the love of my family, and getting that music out there. I knew what I was feeling was so real and I wanted other people to hear it. If we get to sing on the Grand Ole Opry that's great, because more people get to hear the songs and that brings recognition to my dad and to God's message."[7]

During times when music bookings were scarce, Tammy sought work elsewhere. Like Tammy Wynette, the Grammy Award–winning country music legend after whom she was named, Tammy studied and worked as a cosmetologist in Nashville. But singing the gospel songs of her father was always her career choice.

While some religious denominations mandate male leadership only, Tammy and Jerry serve as co-leaders within their ministry.

Tammy and Jerry Sullivan on stage ca. 1979. L-R: unknown bassist, Tammy Sullivan, Jerry Sullivan. Photograph courtesy of Tammy Sullivan.

While Jerry offers his testimonies as precursors to songs, Tammy's testimonies are often embedded within the songs written by Jerry or by Jerry and Marty Stuart for Tammy to sing.

"I think whether you're a woman or a man," says Tammy, perhaps drawing inspiration from the Parable of the Talents, "if God gives you a gift, He wants to use you. I think you should be allowed to do it. I believe He's given me the gift to sing gospel songs and the songs Daddy writes. I believe He set us on this road. If He gives you the gift, I think you should be allowed to use it. Anywhere."

Jerry agrees. "I do, too. I don't think God looks at us as male and female. He looks at us as His children."

"As a servant," adds Tammy.

"As a servant," Jerry echoes. "Like she said, we're on a mission and she's our vocalist. She lives these songs as she sings them, you know."[8]

For the Sullivans, being "real" is a recurrent theme in their testimonies and a quality they regard as defining their music and ministry. In his introductory remarks in concert, Jerry often tells the audience that what they are about to hear is "real." Jerry means their music and testimony is authentic, and he and Tammy believe in and try to live according the Biblical values expressed in their songs.

The Sullivans' songs are characterized by their positive, uplifting messages of hope, redemption, and salvation. The Sullivans don't sing or preach the hellfire and damnation theology favored by some evangelists. Rather, they offer to their audience empathy born of their own emotional wounds and belief that, no matter what errors one has committed in his or her life, Jesus is the path to redemption.

"When I was growin' up," Tammy says, "I lived the pain and the disappointments when maybe the trips didn't turn out exactly like they wanted it—they didn't make enough money for all the families to have everything they needed. And the disappointments of my father not bein' there when I needed him. Like if it's bad weather, you want Daddy there. We lived way back in the woods, and it was just me and my mom; we were there by ourselves a lot of times when I wanted my Daddy. And events at school, when I was little, and he wasn't able to be there because he was on the road. Things like that. And I *lived* this, I went through it, and it just projects out in what I'm singin'. That's why I like the songs *he* writes. I can feel those songs because I know they're *real*."[9]

While the Jerry and Tammy sound is more contemporary than the old-time gospel of Enoch and Margie, Tammy feels honored that she and her father are a part of the Sullivan tradition that began in the 1940s.

"I think my family took a way of life and an upbringin', and they dedicated their lives to it," she says. "I think they said, 'We might not have a lot of material things or a big education, but we were shown a lot of love and honesty and hard work.' They took it into the South and into our community.

"I can tell there was a road paved before me. When I get [on stage], people know what our music is about. There's always been a standard. People will tell me, 'My mom listened to the Sullivan Family all her life; she brought me when I was a little girl.' My family has carved out a place where people respect our music and respect our lives."[10]

It was Victory Grove Church that nurtured Tammy from a young age. For Tammy and her extended family of aunts, uncles, and cousins, church was a form of entertainment as well as spiritual enrichment. Washington County hadn't changed much since the days of Aunt Elva's childhood. "There wasn't many places around here where you could go," Tammy says. "So church was the main place for me. We would have the best times goin' to church. That's what I looked forward to. I didn't get up and sing back then, but I loved to listen. The music is what drew me into church. I learned how to sing harmony. What was so funny is there was nothing for anybody else to do, so everybody just went to church. That was what we did.

"My cousin Myra [Aunt Suzie's daughter] would go to church with me. Myra took care of me a lot of times because when I first started goin' to church, my dad would be playin' with Uncle Enoch and them and they didn't make hardly any money. Our income was low. I remember not havin' a lot of clothes to wear to church, but Myra would always make sure I had the right stuff to wear. She and Aunt Susie would buy me things to wear. It was rough back in those days financially. When daddy worked with them, I think his income was $50 to $75 a week.

"There's something about when your family sticks by you. Like Myra and Brother Glenn and all of us goin' to church, we had that church thing goin' so it really didn't matter to me. I knew if I was taken care of, God was gonna take care of me. But we had a lot of fun and a lot of love. All the stuff I didn't have, I didn't notice so much."[11]

After her uncle Arthur's death, Theo Wilson became pastor of Victory Grove Church. Tammy credits Brother Theo for facilitating her spiritual quest. "We all loved Brother Theo. The main reason was he didn't preach too long. His sermons were short and sweet. And every church night, he would invite people—if you didn't have the Holy Ghost, that was the main thing with him. He believed if you didn't have it you didn't go to Heaven. Every one of us got the Holy Ghost right there. I was an eleven-year-old.

"A lot of it, I think, was the way Brother Theo preached. He would always give that altar call and that drawin' thing: 'You'll know when God's dealin' with ya. You answer his call.' I knew God was dealin' with me and I'd been knowin' it for some time. I had went to the altar before, but I had never received the Holy Ghost."

According to Holiness-Pentecostal doctrine, the physical manifestation of Spirit Baptism is glossolalia—speaking in tongues. As recorded in Acts 2 Chapters 2–4, on the Day of Pentecost: "And suddenly there came a sound from heaven as of a rushing mighty wind, and it filled all the house where they were sitting. And there appeared unto them cloven tongues like as of fire, and it sat upon each of them. And they were filled with the Holy Ghost, and began to speak with other tongues, as the Spirit gave them utterance."

"I know I did speak in tongues that night," Tammy says. "It was awesome. It was like a thousand pounds lifted off of my shoulders. When I finally surrendered and turned my life over to God, it was like I knew I was makin' a change for the better. Everybody was happy for me. All my family and friends came around me and were all prayin' for me. Tears and everything. It's something you seek—I had been to the altar many times before. When it happened, it was very easy because all I had to do was surrender everything to God.

"My life got God-directed in a big way. I started becoming more aware of the things God wanted me to do. I could feel his presence with me all the time. There's a difference between believing in God and havin' Him inside of you and His presence with you. Hearing His thoughts, and being able to work through me. I could tell God was beginning to work through me. I know He did because I came home and lived my life in front of my parents. And neither one of them was in church. After that, my Dad started goin' to church with me."

Tammy says she and her father played in charismatic churches where people prophesize, speak in tongues, roll in the aisles, and so on. "People are *very* close," she says. "They know each other and their problems and pray for individuals in close prayer groups. People wail and tears flow. It's like group therapy."[12]

As an adult, Tammy experienced the disappointment of failed marriages. In 1984 she married J.R. Johnson. J.R. ("Junior") played keyboards with Jerry and Tammy, and appears on their 1988 audio cassette *Authentic*. The marriage produced one child, Trey, before dissolving in 1989.

In 1992 Tammy married Aubrey Lee Williams, a fellow graduate of Leroy High School. They divorced the following year. Eleven years later, when Tammy was long removed from contact with Williams, he was arrested and accused of murdering his wife, Joan Williams. Mrs. Williams was found deceased with ten bullet holes. Mr. Williams had a gunshot to his left thigh. At the hospital, his blood alcohol level registered .257. In court, Mr. Williams pled self-defense. The jury did not believe him, and he was sentenced to forty-two years in Alabama State penitentiary.[13]

Tammy found love again in 2001, when she began dating her friend, Jonathan Causey. Causey was born in 1967 in bayou country of Mamou, Louisiana, and grew up in nearby Lake Cove. He first met the Sullivans in 1982 when they performed at Brother David Messer's Happy Hollow Holiness Church in Lake Cove. Causey grew up in a gospel music family and was interested in a gospel music career. He spent the summer of 1984 living with Jerry and Zelma, before returning home to finish his last year of high school. Brother David generously provided Jonathan with a mandolin. The Sullivans' cassette recording *Authentic* was twenty-year-old Jonathan's first experience in the recording studio.

Jonathan married in 1992, and he and his wife made the rounds as a gospel act. Their daughter, Savanah, was born the following year. Jonathan divorced in 2000, and was driving trucks and doing roofing jobs when Tammy phoned. "Tammy called me up and encouraged me about my music," Jonathan recalls. "She told me God had a purpose, that He had something for me to do. She invited me to join them for a show in Birmingham."[14] Other shows followed in 2001, and Jonathan and Tammy began dating. They married in 2002.

In 2004 Tammy gave birth to their son, Jon Gideon Causey. Jonathan became a full-time member of the Sullivans' gospel band, playing guitar, mandolin, and singing his father-in-law's songs. In 2017 Tammy succumbed to cancer. Jonathan became a single parent, homeschooling Jon Gideon and teaching him to play music and sing in the gospel tradition of the Sullivans. As a teen, Jon Gideon began sharing the stage with his father. In 2020 they released their first CD, *The Greatest Story*. Singing songs written by his grandfather and sung by his mother, Jon Gideon carries the legacy forward, the fourth generation of Sullivans to travel the gospel highway from south Alabama to Louisiana and the world beyond.

*Chapter 7*

# Traveling the Gospel Highway from Potholes to Praise

The faint pink glow of south Alabama's dawn slips through the curtains of the Sullivans' mobile home as Jerry and his wife Zelma rise to greet the day. It's 6:00 a.m., and within a few hours, Jerry, Tammy, Jonathan, Chad Maharrey, and I will begin the 300-mile, six-hour journey from Wagarville to Ball, Louisiana, where the band will play the first of three weekend church jobs.

The Sullivans haven't worked much in the past year. Tammy gave birth to Jon Gideon. The infant was born with spina bifida, requiring Tammy's attention at home and frequent trips to medical specialists in Birmingham. The cost of medical care and the loss of performance income have imposed a strain on the Sullivans' finances, and Jerry has scaled back on expenses. His Silver Eagle tour bus sits idle in a nearby lot, a "For Sale" sign propped against the windshield. Jerry says operating the bus was burdensome, citing the high cost of maintenance and escalating price of diesel fuel for a vehicle averaging 6.5 miles per gallon on the open road. Besides, at his age it's difficult to maneuver the clunky Silver Eagle in and out of tight parking spaces, the only kinds available at most Sullivan gigs. Last week, Jerry traded in his 1996 maroon Cadillac Deville for a silver

2002 model, and that's how he and I will travel to Louisiana. Tammy and Jonathan will ride in their car. Chad, a multi-instrumentalist and occasional bandmate, will drive his pickup truck, his girlfriend beside him in the cab.

Aside from comfort, there are advantages to traveling to gigs in the spacious confines of a tour bus. It enables the bandleader to know the whereabouts of his bandmates at all times. If the bus breaks down or arrives on time, everyone shows up at the venue together. Traveling separately introduces an infinite number of uncertainties which may affect Jerry as bandleader and the fans in their expectations of what they hear on stage. But on this trip, separate vehicles are required.

With a light load of clothes, a suitcase filled with CDs, and Jerry's guitar secure in the trunk, we exit the Sullivans' driveway and turn toward Chatom, where Jerry has arranged to meet Chad at Bertile's Biscuits and Burgers at 8:30. The plan is to drive to Louisiana in tandem in case one of the vehicles breaks down along the way. But it's 9:30 now, and Jerry and I have been sharing a small table at Bertile's, sipping coffee and waiting for Chad to show. Finally, Jerry grows impatient and decides to go on without him; we head across the street to gas up at the Jordan Mini-Mart. Suddenly, as if on cue, Chad arrives in his pickup truck, his girlfriend beside him in the cab. Chad tells Jerry he's been unable to cash a check he earned last week from singing at a Baptist church, and that he needs to drive to his main bank branch in Mobile before heading to Louisiana. Agitated, Jerry informs Chad that a side trip to Mobile will make him late for tonight's job. He offers to pay for Chad's gas by credit card and to advance him money for hotel expenses.

Nerves taut because of the delay, Jerry is concerned he hasn't heard from Tammy and Jonathan. He tried phoning them earlier, but there was no answer. His younger daughter, Stephanie, has driven to Tammy's house, and will call home to Zelma when she arrives. Chad will call Zelma on his cell phone, and relay the message to Jerry at the first rest stop. It's 10:25. We left Wagarville two hours ago, and have driven a mere fifteen miles. Jerry turns to me and says, "I put up with pure torture because I believe I'll be rewarded down the line. It may be after this life, but I believe I will."[1] Jerry eases the car onto Highway 56 toward the Alabama-Mississippi state line, Chad and his girlfriend trailing behind.

I enjoy these trips with Jerry. The long hours together allow time to renew our friendship and to catch up on family news. They also provide the opportunity for me to ask Jerry questions without the interruptions that invariably arise when we are at his home in Wagarville. These road trips are special times which I value as one-on-one tutorials with my favorite "professor." I am Jerry's student, and I listen intently, tape machine on "record," as he teaches me the finer points of his music, faith, and life.

We're not far outside Chatom when the conversation turns to songwriting. Renowned for his uplifting songs of hope and inspiration, Jerry writes most of the songs he and Tammy sing. In 1993 the Country Music Hall of Fame in Nashville, Tennessee, mounted an exhibit displaying Jerry's song manuscripts, his Bible, and other personal belongings. It was the first time the Hall had devoted an exhibit to a gospel songwriter and performer.

Jerry has eighty-eight songs registered with the music licensing organization BMI. He has written solo and collaborated with others, including Tammy and Kathy Louvin, daughter of Ira Louvin of Louvin Brothers fame. I'm curious to know where he finds the inspiration to write songs as varied as the Cajun-flavored narrative "The Jesus Story," the rockabilly-style ballad "The Old Man's Prayer," and the hard-charging bluegrass gem "Brand New Church." I want to know if the songs are born of personal experience, or if they come to him at times in dreams. The late bluegrass artist John Hartford claimed to have written the folk-pop classic "Gentle on My Mind" in fifteen minutes upon waking from a dream after seeing the film *Dr. Zhivago*. Similarly, Townes Van Zandt, composer of "Pancho and Lefty" and other country hits, said that the melody and words to "If I Needed You," recorded by Emmylou Harris and others, came to him in a dream.

Jerry tells me how he wrote his first song, "I Can See God's Moving Hand," in 1949, when he was fifteen years old. Working in a sausage factory in Tampa, Florida, he got the idea for the song from hearing sermons by a preacher who was part of the revival that swept through America in response to the twin threats of communism and the atomic bomb. He explains that "Brand New Church" was written to celebrate the reunification of his home church following a schism that threatened to destroy it. "The Jesus Story" was inspired by watching a holiness minister, John Scroggins, preach amid the glow of an oil lamp while fighting off a mosquito swarm from the stream below. Brother Arthur was too sick to walk to the preaching, so Jerry carried him there in an oxcart. And Jerry tells me his most recent song, "Shadow of the Steeple," reminds worshippers to embrace the homeless and addicted who often reside in doorways or under bridges within sight of stained-glass cathedrals.

Jerry's song are simple, often three-chord structures that extol Christian principles of righteous living and moral rectitude. The listener may easily identify with the messages in Jerry's songs, having heard them echoed from pulpits and harmonized in churches favoring songs from old-time shape-note hymnals. Jerry does not adhere to strict theological orthodoxy, nor is his music driven by a notion of bluegrass purity. This libertarian flair imbues his songs with broad appeal as he feels free to draw upon elements of the blues, rhythm and blues, Cajun, African American gospel, and bluegrass idioms.

When Tammy joined her father in his ministry, his songwriting changed from Enoch-and-Margie traditionalism to songs more attuned to Tammy and her generation of gospel fans. "The music the Sullivan Family sang starting in 1949 was traditional," Jerry says. "When Tammy came along, there was youth again. She made me hear things I needed to write about to involve her. I think my songs got deeper, and my walk with the Lord got stronger."[2]

Marty Stuart first met Jerry when the Sullivan Family opened a gospel show by Bill Monroe and His Blue Grass boys in Jackson,

Alabama. Marty was eleven years old. Jerry Sullivan was playing bass and sang his composition "The Born Again Experience."

"He tore the house down," Stuart recalls. "It was rock and roll. He had the rhythm, he had the spark. They all had charisma, but Jerry had an extra something. After the concert, I made a beeline to the Sullivan table to get a copy of 'The Born Again Experience.' "I got Jerry to sign it. He took my hand and said, 'You want to be a musician, don't you?' I said, 'Oh, yes sir!' He said, 'Well, you've got what it takes. You just hang in there and keep on playin." It was like a wink, a knowing of things to come."[3]

In 1972 Enoch and Margie invited Marty and his friend and fellow Mississippian, Carl Jackson, to join the Sullivan Family Gospel Singers for the summer tour. It was Marty's first professional experience and set the stage for his tenure with Lester Flatt and the Nashville Grass. Stuart's relationship with Jerry Sullivan endured, and he and Marty began to write gospel songs together in the late 1980s. Stuart's career in bluegrass, country, and gospel music endows his music with rich melodic and rhythmic textures. Together, Jerry and Marty have crafted enchanting songs including "Tomorrow," "At the Feet of God," and "Praise the Lord for this Life I'm Livin'," sung by Tammy.

"We wrote our first song about 1988 or 89," Marty says. "It was on the way to Carthage, Mississippi. I was down-and-out, going through a divorce and lost record deal. Jerry was needing a mandolin player for a tour, so I drove to Jug's house, got on his bus and went to sleep. When I woke up we were on our way to Carthage to a singing that night.

"I'd been playing Bill Monroe's mandolin instrumental called 'Get Up John' in my head a lot. I always knew Jerry was a great singer and a great guitar player and bass player, but his songwriting is what set him apart. He was the Bernie Taupin of the Sullivan Family Gospel Singers. He was responsible for a lot of that body of work. I always wanted to write with him.

"So I got up on the bus and I played it for him and I said, 'I always wanted to hear words with it about John the Baptist.' That was the first song. We wrote two or three more songs on that trip. This twenty-year avalanche now has come. Any time we get together, God blesses us. We used to laugh and hope that we don't run out of paper, because they come fast and furious when we do that together."⁴ Jerry and Marty took Bill Monroe's hard-driving instrumental and made it a hard-driving gospel song. Emmylou Harris recorded their version of "Get Up John" on her 1992 live CD *At the Ryman*.

"I could not write the kind of gospel songs that come out of me without Jerry," Marty allows. "There's a great spark in him. He's wonderful to write out of the Old Testament with because it's his language, it's his understanding. Every word has been garnered, every word has been lived through and lived out, and you can't beat that kind of experience. And, he lives what he's singing. He lives what he's believing. He throws it all on the line, every single day. You can't beat that kind of living."⁵ We cross the Mississippi River into Vidalia, Louisiana, and pass an assortment of churches along the main thoroughfare: Apostolic Life Temple, Vidalia Church of Christ, Baptist Bible and Book House, Faith Tabernacle, Apostolic Pentecostal Church. Modest cinderblock restaurants serve boiled crawfish and hand-lettered signs tacked onto telephone poles advertise jumbo shrimp, $5.95 a pound.

Heading west on State Road 28, cotton fields with newly planted seedlings recede into the horizon, their white, fluffy bolls radiant against the rich, black soils of the alluvial plain. Jerry calls this stretch of highway a "swamp road." When he first traveled here with Brother Arthur in the 1950s, it was paved with gravel and subjected to frequent inundations. Today, it's built on fill elevated above the floodplain. Jerry and Bill Monroe hunted fox together in the nearby fields.⁶

A metal sign welcomes us to Ball, Louisiana, and exhorts the visitor to "Attend Church Faithfully." We stop at Paradise Grocery, across the road from Paradise Catfish Kitchen. Jerry uses the grocery's pay phone and calls old friends Wayne and Margaret Sweat for directions to their home. They direct us along a two-lane road between the restaurant and store. Around 4:30, Jerry and I pull up to the Sweats' home while the rest of the band checks into a local motel. Jerry has known Margie Sweat, née DeVille, since the 1950s, when she and Jerry's nephew Emmett dated. The Sweats have invited us to stay with them while we're in the area. Some years earlier, the Sweats gifted Jerry the Martin D-28 guitar he uses to this day. The visit is an opportunity to renew friendships, and it relieves the financial burden of paying for an additional motel room. After a modest but nourishing meal of ham and turkey sandwiches and potato salad, Jerry lies down for a half-hour nap before readying himself for the evening's singing.

*Friday May 27, 2005*

The Lighthouse Chapel of Tioga is a sprawling tan brick building next door to Wade's Transmission Service in Rapides Parish. Across the street, rusted automobile axles and abandoned truck cabs lay surrounded by patches of white Queen Anne's lace and blue-flowered chicory. By 6:30, the audience begins arriving in an assortment of dented pickup trucks and older model sedans. These are typical Sullivan fans: Hard working, middle-class Christians, many of whom have followed the Sullivans since the early days with Brother Arthur.

Following a brief introduction and opening prayer, the Sullivans begin the concert at 7:05. The audience of sixty-five persons is about half the number that can be accommodated by the church's seventeen wooden pews. The audience is a graying crowd, with a few children squirming restively on their mothers' laps. On the wall behind the band, a bulletin board announces the church's recent history:

| | |
|---|---|
| Attendance Today | 31 |
| Attendance Last Sunday | 34 |
| Offering Today | 142 |
| Offering Last Sunday | 24 |
| Attendance Year Ago | 28 |

## *Pastor C. Pat Carrington*

Brother Carrington, a burly, plain-speaking man of forty-three, follows in his father's footsteps as a licensed minister of the United
Pentecostal Church. He describes himself as "old-time Pentecostal,"
by which he means he adheres to "the old-time doctrine, the apostolic doctrine, the way the apostles preached it."[7] Brother Carrington's
ministry hasn't been without controversy. In the past four years, two
of his churches have been burned to the ground by what he calls
"mentally disturbed church members." In the sixteen months he's
led Lighthouse Chapel, he hasn't enjoyed much success growing the
church's rolls which, he says, number some "forty active members."
There's a strain of frustration, perhaps even despair, in his voice as
he talks about his struggles.

"We've had probably in the past year 250 people come through
this church," he says, looking out from behind the large oak desk in
his office. "When they learn the doctrine, they don't stay. They think
it's cultish, to be honest with ya." The pastor is especially discouraged
by what he sees as a trend toward moral relativism, and by younger
members of the congregation who, he says, expect services to be as
much about entertainment as salvation.

"There are so many churches around this part of the country
that's turning away from the apostolic way of teaching—the old-
time teaching and holiness. It's got to where you can just about do
anything you want to and still go to heaven. What used to be a sin
is no longer a sin! Nowadays, they can smoke and drink, and on
service nights just ask God to forgive 'em and it's all over with. But
I think God gets tired of that.

"I preach and teach the Acts 2:38, the old-time Spirit Baptism.
Baptize in Jesus' Name, speakin' in tongues to initially receive—as
the evidence of receivin' the Holy Ghost. The younger group just
don't believe that anymore. And if you're not jumpin', runnin', and
shoutin' through the whole service, they don't want no part of it.
They don't like the teachin' part of it. If I brought in a real spirit-filled

bunch of singers that's givin' it everything they got—this hoorah-type singin'—I could fill this church up every Sunday morning. But we still hold to the old-time singin'. Just like tonight."[8]

The Sullivans close the concert with a full-throttle rendition of the gospel classic, "Working on a Building." The song, which some consider "the Pentecostal Anthem" for its lyrical reference to "a Holy Ghost building," sends the audience home with an emotional uplift, and may prompt some to visit the CD table which Tammy has set up near the exit. By 9:30, the sanctuary is nearly empty as the band loads the last of the microphone stands and instruments into their vehicles. Tammy visits with fans in the vestibule where she's been tending to CD sales, while Jerry rests in the back pew. I ask Brother Carrington to evaluate tonight's performance, and how he feels about the Sullivans' ministry.

"I feel the spirit of God behind their singin'," he says. "Anointing, let's put it that way. I feel the anointing on their singin'. It's not a show. There's a lot of entertainers, and then there are people who sing from their heart. The Sullivans sing from the heart."[9] Brother Carrington hands Jerry a check and we exchange our respective goodbyes.

"That was a poor church," says Jerry, as we leave the parking lot and head back to the Sweats', where we'll eat a late supper before turning in for the night. The promoter who arranged this tour told Jerry the band should collect $500 from each church. But tonight's offering totaled $350, which would be shared by Tammy and Jonathan, Chad, JP, and Jerry for food, gas, and salaries.[10] Hopefully, tomorrow's singing will bring better pay.

*Saturday May 28, 2005*

Jerry grows silent as we turn onto the dirt driveway leading to the Tree of Life Tabernacle in rural Colfax. Surrounded by a hardwood copse fifty yards from the rural two-lane sits a white single-wide house trailer with a cross nailed above the front door. A few

Tree of Life Tabernacle, Colfax, Louisiana, 2005. Photograph by Jack Bernhardt.

men and women mill around outside, greeting folks who arrive in Dodge pickups and Chevy sedans with American flag decals and Support Our Troops ribbons adorning their trunks and tailgates as public announcements of their patriotism. One bumper sticker reads, "Heaven Is Real. Do You Have Reservations?"

Inside the trailer-church, the twelve-foot-wide interior is casual and snug. Seven narrow plywood pews, each wide enough to seat two or three worshippers, are arranged on each side, separated by a narrow, carpeted aisle. If necessary, the addition of a few folding chairs can raise the seating capacity above the number accommodated by the pews.

Brother Wayne Howell and his wife, Gayla, have led Tree of Life Tabernacle for about a year. He says that between five and twenty-five members, most of them senior citizens, attend Sunday services. A Jesus Only minister licensed through the Full Gospel Church of Alabama, Inc., Brother Howell is saddened by the recent loss to a heart attack of the gentleman who built the church's pews. "I've got a horse trough back of the church I baptized ten people in," he says, explaining how the man was saved shortly before he died. "He had an artificial leg which he took off and he stepped into the water for the baptism."[11]

A deejay at a local radio station, Brother Howell sports a towering coif of graying black hair, slicked back in a style reminiscent of the Pentecostal evangelist Jimmy Swaggart. And like Swaggart, Howell has recorded a CD of some of his favorite compositions, including the Sullivans' signature song, "Sing Daddy a Song." He tells the audience he recently learned the song was written by Jerry Sullivan.[12]

At 7:10, the band crowds onto the cramped altar, the musicians maneuvering their bodies and instruments delicately into position. At six feet six inches high, the ceiling offers barely enough room for Tammy to wield her tall, bulky bass fiddle, yet somehow everyone manages to find their space. Brother Howell steps to the microphone and welcomes the audience—twenty-seven fans, including the Sweats and their friends Sylvia and Jessica.

"How many feel's like payin' a good love offering tonight?" Brother Howell asks in a tone that's more demand than request. "That's what I want to know. I don't hear ya." Brother Howell steps away from the microphone and walks a few feet into the audience where he makes a rambling, impassioned appeal:

"Let me say somethin'. I work on the radio and I'm not gonna embarrass Brother Jerry. I've worked in the church for a long time, and they say these are 'love offerings,' but the audience don't love 'em, 'cause when they get through takin' 'em up they don't come up with—ya gotta figure it out—he gave a dollar, he gave fifty cents. God'll bless ya if ya give.

"Brother Jerry comes to glorify God. But a man don't work, he don't eat. I'm not gonna get up here like they do at a camp meetin' and say, 'Who's gonna give a thousand dollars?' But I think we should give him a decent offerin'. Can somebody say Amen?" (A subdued shout of "Amen" drifts in unison through the trailer.) "Clap your hands!" the pastor exhorts, and the audience applauds. Brother Howell presses the play button on a CD player at the rear of the altar, and he begins to sing "I'll Fly Away," accompanied by organ music. The audience sings along, clapping hands in time with the organ, which bears more resemblance to roller rink music than a Jimmy Swaggart revival.[13]

Following a prayer by Brother Howell's father-in-law, the pastor introduces the band, which is missing its banjo and guitar player, Chad. "We're glad to be here and take part in this service," Jerry begins. "And we want you to enjoy our songs. We had a good service last night. The mainest thing about these things is, it's real with us. We travel and sing and carry a message that we want people to hear. And I'm gonna have a good time! I want you to join me, if you will. If you can't, just set there," Jerry says, breaking into his warm, welcoming laughter.

"We're still missin' one of the group. He's on his way. We went to a big barbecue down in Bunkie, and I reckon he's still eatin' barbecue down there. Brother David Messer and his family, I think they're on their way here, I guess, with Chad. We gonna be right here enjoyin' the blessin's of the Lord." Jerry nods to his band, and together they kick into gear with a snappy version of the classic "Crying Holy unto the Lord."[14]

The concert has been underway for twenty minutes when Chad arrives and rushes to the stage to join in on Jerry's showcase guitar instrumental, "Gloryland March." The arrival of Chad's girlfriend, along with David and Tricia Messer, their children and grandchildren, boost the audience to thirty-seven persons. We had spent the afternoon at the Messers' home in Bunkie, where Brother David and family hosted a barbecue dinner in the Sullivans' honor. With Happy Hollow Holiness Church closed now, the Messers have left Lake Cove and live rent-free on a 3,500-acre ranch in exchange for tending the owner's horses and cattle. The older boys take to their chores like grizzled cowboys on the Chisholm Trail, patrolling the ranch in an ATV with six-guns holstered at their waists and rifles at the ready. While kids elsewhere entertain themselves with skateboards and X-Box games, the Messer boys get their thrills by helping to keep the residents of Avoyelles Parish safe from snakes and alligators. Brother David was the first minister to hire Jerry and Tammy when they began their ministry in 1979, and he and his family are among the Sullivans' most loyal friends and supporters. They think nothing of driving for hours to attend the Sullivans' singings, so it's no surprise to see them here tonight.

Jerry and Tammy Sullivan Performing at Tree of Life Tabernacle, 2005. Photograph by Jack Bernhardt.

The singing ends around 9:30. As the band loads out, I share a pew with Brother Howell, who tells me about his ministry and his congregation. "The folks that come here are mediocre people," he says, meaning they are ordinary, working-class, and poor. "They live from paycheck to paycheck. I ain't braggin'—this is between me and you," he says, leaning toward me as he lowers his voice to a near-whisper. "We got $141 tonight. I know Jerry's been doin' it a long time. I'm a givin' person. I put that other $271 in to get that $412 offering. That's the kind of person I am. God's gonna bless me sometime. I don't know how."[15]

On the way back to the Sweats, Jerry rides along in silence, contemplating the pros and cons of the evening's event. Without criticism or complaint, he turns to me and says, "That was the smallest church I ever carried a group into."[16]

*Sunday May 29, 2005*
We arrive at Lonestar Pentecostal Church at 2:00 p.m., at the conclusion of Sunday services led by the pastor, Bishop Calvin Robinson. Bishop Robinson is not familiar with Jerry and Tammy Sullivan, but he has heard of Chad's family, the Maharreys, who enjoyed a gospel

hit in the early 1990s with "Jesus Can Heal Your Achy Breaky Heart," a song which derived its inspiration from Billy Ray Cyrus's country smash "Achy Breaky Heart." Bishop Robinson invited the Sullivans to perform today as a favor to his friend, Wayne Howell, who had arranged this and the other church singings on this tour. With its red brick façade and stained-glass windows, Lonestar Pentecostal's architecture is more reminiscent of a Southern Baptist church than a Pentecostal one. The sixty-one-person congregation sits attentively as Bishop Robinson incorrectly introduces the musical guests as "James and Tammy Sullivan, from somewhere in Alabama."

"Wagerville," shouts a member of the audience, mispronouncing the name by softening the "g," making it sound as if it were the casino capital of Alabama. The unfamiliarity with the Sullivans' names and their home town is symptomatic of the often anonymous nature of their ministry. In spite of their Grammy nomination, *Grand Ole Opry* appearances, and accolades from the national press, Jerry and Tammy remain largely unknown throughout most of America. Toward the end of the concert, Bishop Robinson introduces Chad Maharry as "Chad Mahoney," and asks the band if they will play "Jesus Can Heal Your Achy Breaky Heart." His request is ignored.[17]

When the singing ends, the band joins the audience for lunch in the fellowship room. The pastor hands Jerry an envelope containing $350. After a quick meal, the musicians head for the parking lot to begin the long trek home. Jerry and I will arrive at his trailer sometime after midnight on Memorial Day.

On Memorial Day afternoon, Jerry and Zelma inventory the CDs and tabulate the income from the weekend's performances:

CD and Tape sales = $355
Lighthouse Chapel of Tioga = 350
Tree of Life Tabernacle = 412
Lonestar Pentecostal Church = 350
———
$1,467

The amount earned in love offerings averaged $130 less per church than Jerry had hoped. Of the total, Jerry will deduct the cost of expenses, including fuel, meals, and snacks (Jerry spent $84 on gasoline for his vehicle, alone), and salaries for musicians, including himself. Profits from CDs and tapes will be claimed by Jerry and Tammy. If, after expenses, the remaining proceeds are divided equally, each musician would earn about $300 for the weekend. The tour was not a financial disaster. It was, however, typical of the unpredictable monetary yield of the Sullivans' ministry, a calling impelled by the urge to serve greater than the urge to earn.[18]

*Chapter 8*

---

# Brother Arthur and Brother Glenn
*From Brush Arbor to Victory Grove Church*

Victory Grove Church is a humble house of worship, a rectangular wood-frame sanctuary built by Arthur Sullivan in 1949. On the west side of US 43 in Wagarville, Victory Grove remains the Sullivans' home church and is pastored by Brother Arthur Glenn Sullivan, the youngest of Arthur's nine children. Glenn Sullivan was six months old in 1957, when his father suffered a fatal heart attack while preaching during Thanksgiving weekend at his Bolentown church in neighboring Clarke County. Although he never saw his father preach, Glenn follows in Arthur's footsteps as minister with the Assemblies of the Lord Jesus Christ, and pastor of Victory Grove Church.

"I never got to hear my dad preach in person," Glenn says. "But Brother Jerry has some tapes and I got to hear a radio program. The energy in his preaching and the music is impressive to me. [They] tell me he would take the whole family and set up on the street. He'd say, 'Come on. We're gonna have church right here.' He'd break out the mandolin and they'd start singing. People would come to hear that, and it would give him a chance to preach the Word of God. I feel I'm carrying on the tradition, and feel honored to be part of that."[1]

Glenn's elder brother, Enoch, allows that their father was not interested in becoming an advanced musician. Rather, he used music as a tool to draw people near to his evangelizing. According to Enoch, Brother Arthur used the music "to get the attention of the people. I even told him, 'Daddy, you use the music like a spider uses his web. You get the music goin' and you get the crowd, then you preach to 'em.'"[2]

Gospel music is among the most enduring cultural expressions in the American South, and musical ministries among the most popular means for evangelizing the Gospel. With origins in the Great Revival and camp meetings that stirred the souls of nineteenth-century Southerners,[3] gospel music has evolved into a salient expression of faith. The Sullivans and their audience remain rooted in Southern folk culture and are united through a mutual embrace of a musico-religious tradition originating in the nineteenth century. The importance to rural Americans of gospel music was understood by Bill Monroe, who made songs of faith a key ingredient of the bluegrass music he developed between 1938 and 1945.[4] Following Monroe's lead, most bluegrass bands today and in the past have incorporated gospel songs into their repertoires and some, like the Sullivans, have chosen bluegrass gospel as their sole commercial expression.

Regional studies of gospel music ministries are a valuable source of data for documenting structure and process of cultural traditions in time and space. In his survey of amateur gospel groups in south-central Kentucky, for example, William Lynwood Montell found that between 1900 and 1990, 40 percent of 825 known gospel groups "were familial in their basic composition."[5] With Enoch and Margie, Jerry and Tammy as standard-bearers, family-based bluegrass gospel groups are also an important feature of Alabama's spiritual landscape.[6] Family-centered gospel groups have a long legacy elsewhere in the South, giving rise to such popular acts as the Joe Cook family, Lewis Family, Blackwood Brothers, the Isaacs, and the Happy Goodmans.[7]

Victory Grove Church conforms in most ways to the characterization of "folk religion" and "folk church" Elaine Lawless describes for her Oneness Pentecostal community in Indiana: "Folk religion must be recognized as a traditional religion that thrives with individual, independent religious groups that owe little allegiance to hierarchical powers. Each church shares certain tenets of belief and religious experience with other similar denominational religious groups in the geographic area but develops, from its own traditions, its own order of service, protocol, male/female participation, and group identity."[8]

Victory Grove is a tradition-rich institution awash in family memories and the focus of much family lore. On any given Sunday, the church may draw twenty-five worshippers, twenty of whom may be the Sullivans' consanguineal or affinal kin.[9] Kinship, as noted by anthropologist Patricia Beaver, "is a cultural value, connecting the individual to other people, to land, to community, to history, and to identity."[10] Thus, the church maintains its familial connection to its founder, Brother Arthur Sullivan.

Although the church has received some notoriety outside Washington County in recordings, radio and television broadcasts, and commercial videos featuring Jerry and Tammy Sullivan, Victory Grove is a community-based association of Oneness Pentecostal believers that has developed its own traditions and group identity. The church is affiliated with the Assemblies of the Lord Jesus Christ that licensed Brother Arthur and his son, Glenn, to the ministry. However, concerned that the Assemblies' doctrine of rules was exclusionary, Arthur distanced himself from some proscriptions while continuing to preach its Oneness canon.

Many of Victory Grove's customs derive from Brother Arthur's interpretation of the Bible and his tolerance for behavior that runs counter to rules of the Assemblies. And with Glenn Sullivan minding the pulpit, today's Victory Grove Church enjoys a large measure of continuity with its past. Brother Glenn echoes his father's sentiments regarding the exclusionary effects of arbitrary rules and conditions, and what he calls the "us four and no more" mentality. "A lot of things we have preached," he asserts, "especially in Pentecost, are man-made conditions and commandments of men. If people get Jesus down in their heart, whether they're wearin' makeup or wearin' a bikini, The Lord will convict them. If you just preach at them all the time and hammer them over the head and tell them, 'It's my way or no way,' you're not going to get anywhere. I remember hearin' about my dad. He reached out to whoever. That's what Jesus said, 'Whoever will, let him come.' We believe that."[11]

When conducting service, Brother Glenn stands before the altar, Bible in hand. He may begin by requesting prayer for those who are ill. He asks the congregation to open their Bibles to chapter and verse he will draw upon for the sermon: "If you have your Bible, turn with me to Second Corinthians, hallelujah, Chapter 7, Verse 1." Tonight's sermon, then, centers upon "Having therefore these promises, dearly beloved, let us cleanse ourselves from all filthiness of the flesh and spirit, perfecting holiness in the fear of God." As he preaches, Brother Glenn paces in front and down the aisles. His voice increases in volume and he becomes animated, echoing his father's style of delivery as heard on a tape recording of one of his father's 1957 radio broadcasts. When Brother Glenn receives the "anointing," worshippers are enveloped in his energy field and become participants in, rather than spectators of, today's liturgy. Continuing, Glenn cites Second Corinthians: "The Bible reads, 'Having therefore these promises.' Now, we've got to see what these promises are. Amen. Anytime you see the word, 'therefore,' look and see what it's *there* for. Amen."[12]

Like Brother Arthur, Glenn often invites guest pastors to minister from the pulpit of Victory Grove. A Wednesday night service features the preaching of Brother Wayne, who says he's not a preacher but likes to share what he's learned. He begins by quoting from Timothy 1:3, and speaks of not believing in false doctrines, which he likens to "old wives' tales." He segues into a discussion of what he sees as neglect of parental responsibility in child-rearing resulting in a lack of discipline in and beyond the home. He cites Proverbs 22:6, "Train up a child in the way they should go, and when they grow old they will not part from it." Brother Wayne seems to speak for

Brother Glenn Sullivan Preaching, Victory Grove Church, Wagarville, Alabama (Jerry Sullivan in pew).
Photograph by Jack Bernhardt.

members of Victory Grove in decrying the decay of traditional values and their replacement by symbols of Mammon. "I can remember
in our dining room," he says. We had a big picture of the Last Supper.
People are replacing the Last Supper with a velvet portrait of Elvis.
Or replacing the Last Supper, Uncle Gerrol, with a bulldog playing
poker." He excoriates drug dealers, whom he accuses of "killing off
our youth, like Herod killed all first-born males."[13]

Washington County is infused with a Christian ethos. While
not all residents are church-goers, ample opportunities exist for
those who desire worship. Victory Grove is one of 157 churches
listed within Washington County;[14] that is one church for every
ninety-eight residents. By comparison, the Yellow Pages of the 1992
Nashville, Tennessee, telephone directory lists 871 churches for
Nashville and its suburbs. With Nashville's metropolitan area population around 1.1 million, the "Protestant Vatican" offers approxi-
mately one church per 1,148 residents.

According to the 2000 US census, the percentage of high school
graduates age twenty-five and over in Washington County is 72.3
percent, compared with 75.3 percent for Alabama. Washington

County residents with a bachelor's degree or higher comprise 8.6 percent as opposed to 19 percent for the state. Median household income in the county is $30,815, and $34,135 for the state. And in Washington County, 18.5 percent of persons live below poverty, compared to 16.1 percent for Alabama.

In Mac's pharmacy in nearby Jackson, a casual conversation with a sales clerk reveals a common theme in this part of Alabama. A former member of Brother Arthur's Bolentown Pentecostal church, she tells me how she lost her husband eight years earlier. One afternoon, she and her husband were visited in their kitchen by their son-in-law and his five-year-old son. Without warning, the son-in-law pointed a pistol at her husband, pulled the trigger, and shot him dead. He then turned the gun on himself and committed suicide.

She shares with me a conversation she had with her husband a month before this tragedy. "He had said to me, 'When I'm about to die, will you walk the last mile with me?' Well, I was there for him; I walked his last mile." Stoically she added, in a phrase I had heard Brother Glenn speak in sermon, "God never gives you more than you can handle. I learned that the hard way. I also spent five years in therapy, but my healing is the work of the Lord."[15] Jerry Sullivan expresses a similar sentiment during his testimony at Victory Grove Church. Speaking to the congregation from the altar, Jerry speaks of his belief in God and how he looks to God to help solve his problems. "I don't have the money to pay for help. And it costs $600 to go to school," he says, referring to the tuition he pays for Stephanie to attend University of South Alabama. "I can't afford to go to school, so I turn to God. He helps me solve my problems."[16]

For Jerry and the Mac pharmacy sales clerk, religion helps make sense of their lives and cope with misfortune. For those who do not share the worldview of science, belief in the supernatural as the source of experience may be a therapeutic, healing force. It also provides a moral compass, or guide for behavior, in a world they find increasingly complex, relativistic, and confusing. Religion also may offer an explanation of tragedy (it is God's will), and ease the emotional pain accompanying loss of a loved one (he/she has been called home, and we'll meet again over Jordan).

Washington County has its share of crime. Sheriff William J. Wheat says his office averages eight domestic violence calls per month; two-thirds involve alcohol.[17] Drug use and distribution also occur. "In our rural community, there's not a lot of activities for young people," says Glenn Sullivan. "Alcohol and drugs are two of the biggest problems we deal with."[18] The Sheriff's Report on the front page of the *Washington County News* lists seventy-four drug, thirty-four domestic violence, and thirty-two DUI arrests from January 5 through June 1, 2005.[19]

Church membership may be a way for parents to steer their children away from temptation and trouble with the law, and act as a buffer against severance of family and community bonds resulting from incarceration.[20]

Victory Grove's twelve oak pews can comfortably accommodate fifty to sixty worshippers, although most services draw fewer. On the small altar in front of the pulpit, a Bible is open to Psalm 20:1, "To the chief musician, a psalm of David." In the space behind the pulpit, musicians gather to sing songs of praise. When Jerry and Tammy are off the road, they may be joined by Brother Glenn (guitar) and Glenn's wife, Sister Tammy (leading the singing), and others who bring their instruments and sing. Shape-note hymnals contain old-time tunes such as William M. Golden's 1914 composition "Where the Soul Never Dies" and Albert E. Brumley's 1932 classic "I'll Fly Away." Nonmusicians may also sing along to recorded tracks of favorite hymns. "Music to me sets the stage for the service," says Glenn Sullivan. "You can sing a joyful song and a worship song and it lifts you up. And there are times when the mood of the service is totally different from that. Maybe it's a time when there's sadness. To me, music is very, very important to the service."[21]

Jerry's sister, Susie, compiled a handwritten list of ninety-one songs the Sullivan Family sang at Victory Grove and other venues. The list features lyrics and the family member assigned to sing each

Singing at Victory Grove Church. L-R: Jewel Sullivan, Kathy Sullivan, Norma Ruth Sullivan, Mrs. Glenn Sullivan, Jerry Sullivan, Glenn Sullivan, Ben Cavanaugh. Photograph by Jack Bernhardt.

song, including "Old Camp Meeting Days," "The Little Community Church," and "The Reason We Baptize in Jesus Name."[22]

Victory Grove's homecoming is held Easter weekend. Homecoming is an important ritual for bringing together current and former members of this family-based church, and reaffirming their spiritual genealogy to Brother Arthur. Throughout the year, services are held Wednesdays and Sundays. Brother Glenn quotes frequently from the King James Version of the Bible. Written in an older style English, the language gives Scripture a sort of verbal patina, bestowing upon it the authority and wisdom of antiquity.

In Jerry Sullivan's tape recording of Brother Arthur's radio broadcast, the pastor tells listeners of members of the community who are ill or in need of help.[23] Requesting prayer for church members or their families who are ill, have suffered an accident, or are hospitalized near death is common at Victory Grove services: "I want to pray the Lord will rebuke this off their body." As pastors petition for the bedridden, those recovering from accidents, or families in need of financial assistance, prayer requests function as a community bulletin board sharing news and soliciting care for those in need.

"In our church we're not tryin' to build up a big bank account," says Brother Glenn. "I believe if the Lord blesses you with money you need to use it in His honor. Sometimes there are people who are in a bind financially and we try to reach out to them. You don't have to go to a foreign country to find people that don't have food to eat or to find people that are hurting. It's right here in our community."[24]

It is not uncommon for Brother Glenn to formulate his sermons around social issues. Crime, education, removal of religion from public schools, lack of accountability, marriage, family, and homosexuality are of concern to Brother Glenn and most, if not all, members of his church. Brother Glenn looks to the Bible for passages he may adapt to his pastoral messages.

Glenn works full-time at Olin Corporation in Macintosh, Alabama, twenty miles south of St. Stephens. His work as a man of the cloth is demanding, but Olin allows him time away to tend to his ministry. "I'm blessed with the job," he says, "because I have to preach a lot of funerals. They've always worked with me as far as lettin' me off. They've never refused me, and they let me make up the time."

Singing or preaching the Gospel has been the family business since Brother Arthur blazed the gospel trail. Glenn's uncle, Jerry Sullivan ("Uncle Jug"), remembers Arthur's advice: "My brother had a way of instilling in our hearts that this is the only thing that's worthwhile. We didn't have any factories around here. Some folks lived off the turpentine boxes, chippin' turpentine, or they cut timber. That industry was fadin' out. So what Brother Arthur was trying to tell us is that this is something we could hold on to. 'It's something you can put in your heart and let God work in your life,' Brother Arthur asserted. 'I can't offer you nothing else. I wish I could say, Young 'uns, we'll go get a job somewhere, but Brother Arthur can't do that. But I'll tell you what we can do—we can stick together here and know that every song we sing, every place we go, there is a reward for it.' And he said, 'When I'm gone, if you want to do something special for me, here's what you do. When you have a big get-together, a family reunion or something like that, just get up there and tell 'em I was an old-time preacher man, and I believed in what I was doing. And sing me a song.'"[25]

To honor Brother Arthur, whom he considers his "spiritual father," Jerry composed "Sing Daddy a Song." Arthur's biological son Enoch and Margie recorded the song in 1968. It also appears on Jerry and Tammy's 1990 cassette *Time and Eternity*. The song is performed by Jerry and Tammy at church singings and, per Arthur's request, at Victory Grove's homecoming and other family gatherings:

Let's sing a song for Daddy / He left us a long time ago/
Though it broke our hearts when God called him / He's
    happy in Heaven I know
His parting words when he left us / Remember me when I
    am gone
When you have a family reunion / Please sing Daddy a song

Before Daddy died he taught us / Many gospel songs that
    we sing
And under God's great inspiration / My how his voice
    would ring
He never grew tired of helping / Or correcting us when we
    were wrong
When you have a family reunion / Please sing Daddy a song

Jerry (spoken): He was working so hard when God called
    him / Trying to prepare the way
For us children to sing for Jesus / 'Til we leave here and join
    him one day
He died while preaching a sermon / Telling the sinners to
    turn from their wrong
A great man of God, our Daddy / And we proudly dedicate
    him this song

Through the years, Victory Grove Church has occasionally experienced conflict within its membership. Brother Arthur and Brother Glenn each came under fire for inviting pastors from denominations other than United Pentecostal Church to preach at Victory Grove. Yet, the schism most threatening to Victory Grove's survival occurred when Jerry Sullivan's daughter, Stephanie, was sent home from Wednesday evening service for wearing what the deacon claimed was inappropriate attire. The family refers to these covenants as "bondage," and the incident prompted Jerry and Marty Stuart to compose "Brand New Church."

Tammy speaks proudly of Stephanie's retort to a preacher who demanded the women remove their cosmetics before they took the stage. "She don't mind speaking out at these places where there's a lot of bondage," Tammy says. "Like the preacher that told us to take the makeup off before we played. She said, 'I'll take it off. But I'm going to tell you, it's not really what I want to do. But in order to go ahead and play, I'll do it. But I don't think it's right!' She told the pastor that!"[26]

The dangers of congregational schism are of concern to Jerry and Tammy, as well as Glenn Sullivan. Their testimony frequently speaks against divisiveness and in favor of an ecumenism that invites all sinners to share in the promise of salvation. Jerry's testimony often precedes the performance of "Let Me Walk, Lord, By Your Side," a bluegrass gospel song written by Carter Stanley and recorded by the Stanley Brothers in 1957. Jerry calls it his "prayer song." Its story line sings of a worshipper unwanted at church until the congregation receives word from on high to accept him. The song parallels the banishment Stephanie experienced at Victory Grove, inspiring "Brand New Church."

While specifics of his testimony differ from audience to audience, Jerry's message reminds the listener of the importance of not excluding people because of symbolic expressions of cultural membership. Testifying at Salem Baptist Church in Raleigh, Mississippi, Jerry insists: "The only way God can speak to this community is through His people, is through you. We've got to tell people, 'Come on in. Regardless how you're dressed. If your hair's to your knees, if it's fallin' to the floor. If your hair's shaved—come on in here.' And you point him to Jesus and let Jesus *fix* it! Jesus can fix it! If you don't like the way he's dressed, pray for him, and Jesus will change him!

"Listen, friend," Jerry continues, "I don't want to try to tell the other person how to go to Heaven. I just want the Lord to keep me by His side, and this song says, 'Steer Me on the Righteous Pathway, Let Me Walk, Lord, by Your Side.' Listen, as Tammy sings."[27]

*Chapter 9*

# Trials, Troubles, Tribulations, and Heavenly Rewards

It's 9:30 a.m. on Wednesday, April 21, 1993, as Jerry and I begin loading the bus. This tour will take us to Philadelphia, Mississippi, to a church pastored by Brother Theo Wilson, a longtime friend of the Sullivans and former pastor of Victory Grove Church.

We'll have a busload on this trip. Stephanie will be with us and play keyboards; she will be joined on stage by Tammy, John Paul, and Jerry. Bob Cormier and Jerry will drive the bus. We're on board by 10:00 a.m., as Jerry leads the prayer: "Thank you, Jesus. Bless us this trip. Keep us out of harm's way. Extend the warranty on this bus. Amen." The bus, a 01 model Silver Eagle, was previously owned by Bob Wootton, Johnny Cash's guitarist. Wootton bought it from Tallmadge Lewis, brother of bluegrass musician Little Roy Lewis. Jerry and Tammy have owned the bus since 1987.

Hundreds of thousands of miles later, the Silver Eagle looks, as is sometimes said of horses, "rode hard and put up wet." Cracks radiate across the windshield like spider webs, and frayed carpet and upholstery attest to miles of wear and tear. At the rear of the bus, four bunks serve as a "motel on wheels," and a small dressing room allows the musicians privacy while donning stage clothes, putting on makeup, and fixing their hair for the stage. Mechanically, the bus is generally reliable enough to shuttle the Sullivans to and from gigs. If, that is, God answers Jerry's prayer and extends the warranty.

We head north on Highway 43, and stop at the local Conoco station. Jerry fills the bus with diesel fuel, while Tammy and Stephanie buy coffee and breakfast for the crew. Breakfast this morning consists of oatmeal cream pies, barbecue corn doodles, Diet Coke, and coffee. And Tums, an essential staple of life on the road.

We pull out from Conoco, Bob at the wheel. Veteran road warriors like the Sullivans find ways to stave off boredom from these long, tedious road trips by reading, story-telling, and looking out the windows at scenery they've seen perhaps hundreds of times. Awake now, Tammy and Stephanie ease into their routines, each sister wearing a new cartoon t-shirt bought earlier in the week at Walmart. Tammy sits at the table, reading and taking notes on her Bible. She asks Jerry what Scripture Brother Glenn mentioned in church last Sunday. Jerry directs her to Apostle Paul's letter to the Ephesians on how to live as a Christian. Tammy works back and forth from her Bible to the New International Study Bible. She keeps a daily journal of events in her life, and looks to Scripture to help her understand them. Like the old Reno and Smiley gospel classic, Tammy uses her Bible for her road map. She examines obstacles and tests she has faced, and reviews her journal to gauge her spiritual growth.

Stephanie reads her textbook, doing homework for her class at the University of South Alabama in Mobile. She looks up from her text and tells this anthropologist that one of her professors believes in Darwin's theory of evolution. The Sullivans are biblical literalists, and Stephanie believes the world and all in it was created as presented in the Book of Genesis. I, on the other hand, use Darwin's 1859 classic, *On the Origin of Species*, for my road map, and we enjoy a lively discussion, pro and con.

Jerry hears our conversation and chimes in. "We started teachin' evolution in the schools and no creator. Well, this person grows up

Tammy in bible study on the road, April 1993. Photograph by Jack Bernhardt.

and the next thing they teach is that you can be anything you want to be, that you don't have to answer to anybody, that he can do it himself. That he has no creator and he come from an ape. He's just confused. We went in a direction instead of what I wanted to see and what Brother Arthur started off, was prayer and plenty of it and don't forget it's only through Christ that we're good."[1]

We continue north on US 45 and pass Waynesboro, where we're greeted by a billboard reading, "Here's Hope. Share Jesus Now. Waynesboro Baptist Churches." The bus lurches forward, pitches to the side, and leaps abruptly skyward like a rickety ride at the county fair. Tires and highway hum a droning serenade; air whistles past a torn rubber door gasket, adding a high-pitched shhhhhh to the mix. Tires thump against uneven sections of concrete like an "overserved" drummer hitting all around, but seldom on, the beat.

The bus continues to roll. Bob slips out of the driver's seat as Jerry slides in and takes the wheel, beginning his shift as chauffeur. Jerry is a seasoned road warrior for whom traveling to gigs is as natural as music and breathing, as if he has diesel in his veins. Every mile, every town seems the same to the novice traveler. But for Jerry, each rest stop, crossroad, water tower, roadside café has its own history and set of meanings for Sullivan Family gospel. Jerry passes the time connecting with his past and telling stories triggered by mnemonic cues he spies as he drives.

Jerry has a library-rich catalog of road stories. He delights in their telling like sea stories of a salty sailor, or war tales repeated over and over by weathered veterans at American Legion halls. When Jerry gets rolling, the stories come fast, one after the other. Bob, JP, or Tammy shout requests: "Tell the one about the time Emmett scared Jack Cooke with the rattlesnakes!"

Jerry chuckles impishly, and says, "I wish you'd been in church the night the lady spit her teeth out. She got up to sing and tell us off because of the girls' makeup—how they felt about us. I looked right at her and said, 'Bless her, Jesus.' She went to singin' and her false teeth flew out of her mouth. She just raked them to her with her foot. She reached down and picked them up and put them back in her mouth. She said, 'The old devil's after me tonight, but I'm gonna win anyhow.' I said, 'That's the spirit. Bless her, Jesus!'"[2]

Not all road stories are comical, but the Sullivans seem to find humor in the most daunting trials. Tammy shares one of hers: "We were going to Church of the Lord Jesus in Wildfork. We left home on time and got about sixty miles from the church. We don't have one blowout. We have three blowouts on US 43!" Tammy and Stephanie roll with laughter, amused by the absurdity of the predicament. "We were stopped in the road. We couldn't move the bus because the blowouts knocked the air tank off. We had to flag traffic around us all afternoon. When we got to the church, we were pitch black because we had to put the tires on ourselves." Stephanie howls with laughter at the image of her sister, the makeup queen, preparing to sing about Jesus while looking like a chimney sweep.

Tammy continues, "When we got to the church, this old lady says, 'Brother Jerry needs a haircut.' "I'm thinkin', a haircut is the least of his worries right now." Tammy's voice softens to a murmur. "That was awful," she says. Then there have been times the bus pulled up to a church and the family was sent home because the pastor changed the date without notifying the Sullivans. Or booked a second band for less money, and sent Jerry and Tammy home with empty pockets. Or expected the band to play for less than expenses.

Through all trials, the Sullivans hold fast to their faith, firm in their commitment to sing and testify and minister to their fans. They will be rewarded, they believe, when their earthly journey ends and they stand with Brother Arthur, singing together on streets of gold.

After lunch at Western Sizzlin, we continue our journey to Philadelphia. Our path turns onto Mississippi State Road 19, the route taken by three civil rights workers the night in 1964 they were brutally murdered and buried in an earthen dam. The deaths of James Chaney, Andrew Goodman, and Michael Schwerner shocked the nation and stimulated passage of the Civil Rights Act, signed into law by President Lyndon B. Johnson. We share the haunted highway with logging trucks bowed with the heft of pine logs bound for pulp and saw mills, and with glistening chrome tankers rolling toward chemical plants near the cities to the south. Rain beats against the windshield. The wiper on the driver's side alone is working; it jerks right, then slaps violently left, flicking sheets of rain to the road below. Winds gust heavily, tossing the bus from side to side. Bob slaps a full nelson on the steering wheel and wrestles the ragged chariot to right of centerline.

Tammy and Stephanie begin talking about codes of conduct enforced in some Pentecostal churches and how these rules have been a source of conflict for them over the years. They tell me about the time they were about to take the stage in a Pentecostal church in Florida. The pastor ordered them to remove their makeup and

Sullivan bus, Livingston, Texas. Photograph by Jack Bernhardt.

jewelry before they entered the church. Makeup and other physical adornments are, of course, intrinsic to the stage presence of many performers, a fact lost on the pedantic pastor. They explain how the Assemblies of the Lord Jesus, inspired by 1 Corinthians, chapter 11, requires men to keep their hair short and forbids women to cut theirs.

They recount the time Stephanie was ordered to leave Victory Grove Church when a deacon took offense that she had arrived for services wearing a long shirt untucked over a pair of slacks. The Sullivans call these restrictions "bondage," and feel strongly that they inhibit their ministry and impose inessential limitations on their lives.

"I've noticed even at my home church they have done me that way," says Stephanie of the restrictions placed on behavior. "They've asked me not to wear pants, or don't do this, don't do that. I know how it feels when you don't believe that way, but you have to conform. My shirt was so long it looked like a dress. I was tired and didn't want to dress up for Wednesday night service, so I figured I'd sit on the back pew. And, oh, the church just . . ."

"One man," Tammy interjects.

"One man," Stephanie confirms.

"Well, see," Jerry explains, "we lost people at our church because of this."

"Yeah," says Tammy. "We had to get those traditions out of our church. That just had to be done away with so we could be free in our church."[3]

Getting "those traditions out" of Victory Grove Church meant removing the members who objected to Stephanie's garb. After a period of negotiation, the dissenters left Victory Grove, and the church continued to worship under Brother Glenn.

This incident is remembered as a defining moment in the history of Sullivan family worship. The potential it held for destroying the church Brother Arthur built is recognized by the family and recounted often by Jerry in testimony relating to the purity of worship as opposed to the taint of fashion. It is also the subject of "Brand New Church," one of the Sullivans' most significant and personal songs. Written by Jerry Sullivan and Marty Stuart, the song celebrates the emergence of Victory Grove Church from this potentially destructive episode as the institutional equivalent of a "born-again experience." The song does not mention specifics of the conflict but instead concentrates on the spirit of freedom and unity that characterizes the church with those proscriptions removed:

> We've got a brush arbor meetin' at our brand new church
> Brand new church, brand new church
> Got some old-fashioned singin' and hell-fire preachin'
> Down at our brand new church

Victory Grove's liberal stance on restrictive dress codes contrasts with the community of Jesus Name believers studied by Lawless in Indiana. She writes:

> Women always wear dresses, and the dresses they wear are
> usually of somber colors, fall well below the knees, and have

long sleeves and high necklines. . . . Pentecostal women wear no jewelry or makeup and, because they are not allowed to cut their hair, it either falls down their backs or is piled high on their heads in a 1950-ish "beehive" hairstyle or pulled back in a severe bun. . . . Similarly, Pentecostal men will have shorter haircuts than other men in the community and will be clean-shaven; it is not uncommon for Pentecostal men to sport a "burr" or "flat-top" haircut. Their clothing, too, is recognizable, as they are most likely to "go to town" in black pants, white shirt, white socks and black shoes. Even Pentecostal young men are not likely to wear blue jeans for fashion, although they may actually work in them.[4]

Dress codes, including the ban on jewelry and cosmetics, constitute a signaling system[5] that encodes and transmits messages about membership in the Pentecostal subculture. It should be remembered that Victory Grove Church has followed its own path since the early 1950s, when Brother Arthur acted against Assemblies elders by inviting non-Pentecostal ministers to preach from the pulpit of his church. Within the family, Brother Arthur is remembered as a free thinker who placed the individual's personal relationship to Christ above outward symbols of faith. Arthur's sister Elva Sullivan Powell recalls a conversation with her daughter, Faye: "A branch of holiness—a lot of them didn't want you to cut your hair and they harped on your makeup. My daughter was in third grade. We was coming up the road one day and she said, 'Mother, when I get big I'm going to be a Baptist.' I said, why? She said, ''Cause I want to wear makeup. Miss Smith wears makeup. She's a Christian and she's a Baptist, so that's what I'm going to be.' I said, 'Okay.' So, she asked Uncle Arthur, 'Do you think it's wrong to wear makeup and wear shorts?' Uncle Arthur said, 'Well, baby, I feel like this. How would you feel if you had on your shorts and you had on makeup, and you saw Jesus. What would you do?' And Faye said, 'Run and meet Him.' Arthur said, 'Well, you've got your answer.'"[6]

Arthur's style of leadership contributed to making him an effective cleric within his faithful circle of followers. It also led to conflict with more orthodox members of his congregation. Dissolution and reorganization of church membership is a process familiar to many evangelical Protestants in the South. The fission of Baptist congregations is well-known, and a similar dynamic has been noted among Pentecostals, where "controversy became an institutional means for removing pastors and denominational officials or, failing that, establishing new fellowships. Internal dissension and schism constituted a means for the upward mobility of new leaders, either within organizations or through the creation of new ones."[7]

Marty Stuart's hometown, Philadelphia, Mississippi, is a moderate-sized community with Southern town demographics: The 1990 University of Mississippi census lists its residents as 16,990 White, 4,626 Black, and 3,144 American Indian.[8] The Native Americans are mostly members of the Choctaw Nation who reside on the nearby Choctaw Reservation. As the seat of Neshoba County government, Philadelphia is an enterprising community with an active commercial district surrounding the county courthouse. The infamous brick compound is where seven men were sentenced to prison in 1967 for the murders of the civil rights workers. The courthouse stands stoically at the center of town, greeting passersby with bureaucratic indifference that betrays none of its troubled past. At the rear of the building, diplomatically shielded from the main flow of traffic, Old Glory flies next to the Stars and Bars, a reminder of our tragic national heritage resulting in the South's "Lost Cause." But times have changed, and so has Philadelphia. In 2009 citizens elected the first Black mayor in the city's history.

The bus rolls through town and turns on to Fork Road, a short winding thoroughfare that transects a mixed residential/commercial neighborhood not far from the center of town. Jerry shifts alert, edging forward nervously in his seat as Bob guides the Silver Eagle cautiously into the church's narrow driveway. The Church of the Lord Jesus Christ is a modest rectangular, cinder block structure.

About five years old, it's a new building compared to other churches we've visited. It is also unusual in its split-level architecture, with lower-level offices occupying space beneath the altar.

To the right of the church, a Black-owned auto body shop does a brisk business, judging from the array of wounded vehicles in- and outside the Quonset-type garage. Across the street, a pallet factory churns sawdust into fine-grained grit that blows in gusts into the church parking lot, stinging the face with the brutality of a sandstorm.

The church's marquee announces the evening's singing and Biblical imperative: ACTS 2:38. Brother Theo's church, like Victory Grove, is a follower of the Oneness, or Jesus Only, branch of Pentecostalism, taking its cue from the Book of Acts, Chapter 2, Verse 38: "Then Peter said unto them, Repent, and be baptized every one of you in the name of Jesus Christ for the remission of sins, and ye shall receive the gift of the Holy Ghost."

Brother Theo Wilson is a robust man of the cloth in his mid-sixties. He was saved under Brother Arthur at Victory Grove Church, and served as pastor there following Brother Arthur's death in 1957. In 1981 he and his wife, Rachel, moved to Philadelphia. Sister Rachel sports long hair packed tightly into a bun atop her occiput, and neck-to-floor clothing mandated by the Assemblies of the Lord Jesus Christ.

Originally from Wagarville, she and Theo were married by Brother Arthur at Victory Grove. Sister Rachel recalls the first Pentecostal preaching she heard was by Brother Arthur in the yard outside Bolentown Church in Clarke County. "It was an open-air preaching," she says, but not brush arbor. Sister Rachel tells me the first pews in this church came from Victory Grove Church. She points to horizontal lines across the top of the pews' lime-green cushions, faded from sunlight where they sat against a large bay window at Victory Grove.

JP tunes the piano while Jerry naps in the back of the bus. A car drives up and a family greets Stephanie. The father tells me he's known the Sullivan Family since they first started singing. He says his family attended Brother Theo's first church in Philadelphia, and that Brother Arthur used to preach to him and his congregation.

Two hymnbooks[9] spread out along two rows of six pews each, are written in shape-note style. The cover of *Banner Hymns (Shaped Notes Only)*, published in 1957, is inscribed on the front cover, Bolentown Holliness (*sic*) Church. The bulletin board at the front right of the altar reads "Sunday School: Record Attendance 51, Attendance today 51, Attendance Last Sunday 41, Offering today $38.67, Offering Last Sunday $14.68." The audience of fifty-one for the concert consists of thirty-six adults and fifteen children ages eight months to fifteen years.[10] The concert is underway at 7:00 p.m., and with few variations follows the Sullivans' set church program.

Jerry steps to the microphone and begins by thanking the audience for coming out to hear the Sullivans. Despite assurances that their programs do not involve sermons, Jerry's soliloquy is nonetheless sermonesque: "This is a special time," he begins. "I wanted to come and be with Brother Theo Wilson, a very dear friend and a man of God. He's like part of our family. He went to our church for a long, long time, then he pastored our church. He was just one of us there like he is here. We're glad to be here tonight and to stand up and say a word for Jesus. He is the important one. We want to put Jesus first in our service. If we do that, then we can look for Him to bless. I learned a long time ago that Jesus was not lookin' for a gospel star. He don't need stars. He can take zeroes and make heroes. So just be a humble servant for God, and He will use you. I've been writin' songs for many long years, all the way back to 1949. We'll pick some of those songs and sing 'em for you because there's a sermon in every one of 'em. So listen for what we're tellin' you."

The concert begins with Jerry's composition "I Can See God's Moving Hand," and segues into the up-tempo "I'm Going Home on the Morning Train." Jerry is on guitar, Tammy on bass, Stephanie plays piano, and John Paul is featured on guitar, mandolin, and banjo. As the song ends, Jerry veers from the music program to address friends and family members in the audience. "I want to recognize someone. Roger and Kathy, that's Arthur Sullivan's baby daughter. Her brother and my nephew, Emmett Sullivan, passed away. He gave a lot of his time to the Gospel. We'll dedicate our program to him."

The set list is familiar, varying slightly to feature Jerry's "Bleeding Heart Dove," based on the New Testament story of a dove stained with Christ's blood as he hung on the cross at Calvary, and Stephanie's piano showpiece, "What a Friend We Have in Jesus." Closing the singing with a riveting version of "Working on a Building," Jerry thanks the audience for coming out on Wednesday night. Tammy adds a final word: "When I was a little girl, before I started singin', we went to Victory Grove Church and Brother Theo would always say, 'Now, get up and sing one, Tammy.' I sounded awful, but he and Sister Rachel would say, 'You sound good.' They always encouraged me. I want to say, thank you for that, and I love y'all."[11]

As the Sullivans leave the stage, Brother Theo reminds folks that CDs are available for sale at the merchandise table, and invites folks to attend church Sunday morning and Sunday evening. We leave the church and drive to Walnut Grove, Mississippi, where we will stay the night with Kathy and her husband Roger. In the morning, we'll journey west toward whatever novel disclosures the gospel highway may yet reveal.

*Chapter 10*

# From Lester Flatt to Place of Hope and the Mother Church
## Service and Celebration
## in the Name of the Lord

It's 2:30 a.m., May 28, 1994. Jerry and I begin loading the bus for the 690-mile excursion to Otto, Arkansas. The band will play a two-day festival before heading on to Nashville and the *Roots of Country* celebration. All are aboard by 3:00 a.m., as Bob eases the bus from Jerry's driveway and turns north on US 43.

Tammy and Stephanie retire to their bunks to catch up on sleep. Jerry sits on the step, keeping vigil while Bob drives. Bob is an experienced bus driver, but Jerry's daughters are aboard asleep in trust, and Jerry assures by his conversation and vigilance that Bob will remain alert. As daylight dawns, Jerry moves toward the back and settles into a brown bucket seat. Here, he will nod off, catching as much sleep as possible while being tousled and tossed as the bus pitches and rolls over the worn, battered highway. His struggle continues for more than an hour, eyes periodically open and shut, head knocking against the bus window. This is as close as he will come to sleep until his nap an hour before the show.

Throughout their career, Jerry and Tammy have served congregations of small backwoods churches as their primary audience. They have also performed for diverse audiences in secular settings, including street fairs and festivals, and recreational venues featuring a variety of musical acts and genres. Lester Flatt Memorial Park in Otto, Arkansas, is an RV park and recreation area surrounding a twenty-two-acre lake. The park is named for bluegrass guitarist/vocalist Lester Flatt who, along with banjo great Earl Scruggs, was a member of Bill Monroe's definitive bluegrass quintet of 1945. Flatt and Scruggs departed Monroe in 1948 and formed the Foggy Mountain Boys, the most popular bluegrass band until Flatt and Scruggs went separate ways in 1969.

In 1972 Marty Stuart and fellow Mississippian Carl Jackson joined Enoch and Margie Sullivan for the summer, playing the Pentecostal church circuit. Later that year, thirteen-year-old Stuart became a full-time member of Lester Flatt's Nashville Grass, a position he held until Flatt's death in 1979.

"The first time I saw Lester in person was at Bean Blossom, Indiana, in 1971," Stuart recalls in an article he wrote for *Bluegrass Unlimited* magazine. "I was 12 years old. I looked at the program and found out what time he was playing and I stood by the bus to watch him come out. That old bus was a sight within itself. It looked like a rolling billboard. It said, 'Lester Flatt and the Nashville Grass Sponsored by Martha White Flour.' It was a vision in diesel. I had no idea . . . that within the next year I'd be on that bus. That's where I'd spend the majority of my teenage years. To this day when somebody asks me, 'Where were you raised?" I say, 'in the back end of Flatt's bus.'"[1] The concert is scheduled for 6:00 p.m. Jerry, JP, and Bob are asleep in the air-conditioned bus by 2:00. Tammy sits quietly in her "study chair," alternately reading her Bible, the newspaper, and *The Road Less Traveled*, the pop psychology best seller on love and self-actualization. Like her Bible, the book offers Tammy advice on love and spiritual growth.

Lester Flatt Memorial Park, Otto, Arkansas, June 1994. L-R: JP Cormier, Stephanie Sullivan, Tammy Sullivan, Jerry Sullivan. Photograph by Jack Bernhardt.

Tammy takes a break from reading. Stephanie joins us and we laugh together about the Nashville star system, a monetized public relations artifact symbolized by the meteoric rise of Billy Ray Cyrus and his megahit, "Achy Breaky Heart." The discussion turns to laughter at the mention of the stir Travis Tritt caused in 1992 when he referred to Cyrus and his song as nothing more than an "ass-wiggling contest." Jerry and Tammy opened concerts for Stuart and Tritt on their 1992 No Hats Tour, a poster of which hangs prominently on the wall inside the bus.

At 4:00 p.m., Tammy springs into action and wakes the men to begin setting up the sound system for their show. At home, Tammy is business manager, phoning pastors and festival promoters to set up gigs and arranging contracts. On the road, she serves as road manager, ensuring the pieces are in place for a successful, quality Sullivan concert. Strong and determined, Tammy is the glue that holds the act together at home and on the road.

The audience of 125 persons is a mix of ages, from retirees living the golden years in their gleaming silver Airstreams, to families vacationing at the lake. The setlist is familiar, but veers off course for the Flatt and Scruggs gospel favorite, "Give Me the Flowers (While I'm Living)." After the show, the Sullivans meet with fans who wish to buy CDs or just say hello. A woman around seventy years old approaches Jerry and thanks him for playing "Give Me the Flowers." She tells Jerry her husband died six months ago, and it was his favorite hymn. "I was on the front row, and I just broke down," she says. "That was his philosophy—he wanted the flowers while he was alive. He was one of the finest men God ever created." She shares that she is lonely, and finds comfort in the Sullivans' songs of hope.[2]

We depart the park bound for the next gig, Jerry at the wheel. Jerry is pleased the park paid the Sullivans $1,200 for their appearance. It was a good paycheck for the family, substantially more than their usual takeaway of $300 to $500 from church gigs. We stop at a roadside store for breakfast snacks and coffee, and continue on our way.

Nestled in an aging residential/commercial neighborhood on the outskirts of Columbia, Tennessee, the Place of Hope may seem an odd choice of venues for a live recording featuring Jerry and Tammy Sullivan. Yet, here they are on a chilly January evening in 2007 to record a benefit concert for the Place of Hope, a Christian residential drug and alcohol treatment center founded by executive director Rev. Mike Coupe.

Rev. Coupe was an alcoholic living on the streets of Nashville until he found God, achieved sobriety and devoted himself to helping others find their way from despair to health. He began his work in 1988 with Maury Regional Medical Center in Columbia, before opening Place of Hope in April 2000. The current facility is a sprawling warren of long narrow hallways with offices, meeting rooms, and residential quarters. Sixty-four beds accommodate residents and staff. The center's mission "is to provide excellent alcohol and drug treatment programs and services, temporary shelter for the homeless, and food for the hungry, within a caring, Christian environment."[3] Twelve-step signs to recovery are posted on the walls, along with a prayer for calm and decorum: "Set a guard, O Lord, over my mouth. Keep watch over the door of my lips. Do not incline my heart to any evil thing." Psalm 141:3–4.

Tonight's show has personal meaning for Tammy and Marty. Each had turned to the Place of Hope for support and counseling at times of inner turmoil and dependency. Tonight's concert is produced by Stuart, and will be released as a live recording on compact disc. The proceeds will be donated to the Place of Hope as a "Thank you" to Mike Coupe and his staff for their work helping those who would otherwise be homeless and hopeless.

Rev. Coupe had previously worked with Stuart and the Sullivans, and is impressed with their compassion for the desperate and lost who come to the Place of Hope seeking to break the death grip of despair.

"The Sullivans and Marty were here two years ago," says Coupe. "One of the things about Marty is that he has really assumed the role of looking out for the downtrodden. It's part of the mantle, I think, passed on from Johnny Cash. Alcoholics, drug addicts, and poor people of all kinds he's got a heart for. So does Jerry Sullivan. When they came here before, they blessed us.

"After Hurricane Katrina, our church was trying to figure out a way where we could go down to either Louisiana or Mississippi and try to do something for the people. We called Jerry Sullivan and he took us into their world along the Gulf of Mexico. We took vehicles full of emergency items. Jerry took us right to the streets so we had a chance to minister and fellowship with each other. It was shortly thereafter that Marty got the idea to do a live album with the Sullivans at the Place of Hope."[4] Since their ministry began in 1979, Jerry and Tammy Sullivan have taken songs and testimonies to varied venues. But tonight will be their first concert in a rehab facility, and their first live album.

The audience of residents, their families, and friends grows quiet as the Sullivans take the stage and open the concert with an up-tempo instrumental version of the traditional gospel favorite "Morning Train." At song's end, Rev. Coupe steps to the microphone and welcomes the audience with prayer: "Father, we thank you for being in this place tonight. And may your anointing come upon these musicians in a glorious way, in Jesus' name we pray."

Rev. Coupe is followed by Marty Stuart, who introduces the Sullivans and exhorts the audience to shout, "Let's make a record!" Marty's father, John Stuart, is here tonight. Later this evening, Marty will join Jerry and Tammy on stage for songs he and Jerry wrote together. As the house rings with applause, the Sullivans launch into a medley featuring the Carter Family's "Lonesome Valley" and "Will the Circle be Unbroken," followed by the African American spiritual "Swing Low Sweet Chariot."

Jerry is in good voice tonight, his resonant baritone strong and rangy. As the band's emcee, Jerry introduces the musicians: Tammy on bass and vocals; Tammy's husband Jonathan Causey on mandolin; Chad Maharrey on guitar; and fiddle player Jason Carter, on loan tonight from the Del McCoury Band. Tammy stands attentively beside her father, leaning on her sturdy bass fiddle the way Jerry leans on her for support.

"This is a song that I wrote some time back," Jerry explains. "It's titled 'The Fingerprints of God.' You know, the fingerprints of God is on all of us because it's forgiveness for our sins. And that forgiveness—you bein' able to forgive and I bein' able to forgive is the fingerprints of God. Listen as Tammy sings about it."[5]

When you look at me I know that you will see
The fingerprints of God on me
I have some battle scars and I have fought in Satan's wars
But the mighty hand of God saved me

Jerry's testimonies, like his songs, are based on personal experiences he comprehends through his reading of Scripture. A lifetime of performing for diverse audiences and situations has sharpened his ability to "read" an audience and tailor his concerts to their needs. Introducing the next song, Jerry references a "saving power, a power beyond my power." Jerry understands that recovery programs, such as offered by the Place of Hope and Alcoholics Anonymous, emphasize acceptance of a "higher power" as prerequisite for healing.

Together and alone, Jerry and Tammy have experienced pain and disappointment in their lives. They rely on faith and the Bible as guides to therapy through prayer. Jerry had turned to his brother Arthur and sister, Elva, for wise counsel. With Arthur and Elva gone, Jerry and Tammy may turn to Brother Glenn as their pastor and "father confessor." Their struggles with disappointment and loss have imbued Jerry and Tammy with a strong sense of empathy. *Psychology Today* defines "empathy" as "the ability to recognize, understand, and share the thoughts and feelings of another person. Developing empathy is crucial for establishing relationships and behaving compassionately. It involves experiencing another person's point of view, rather than just one's own, and enables prosocial or helping behaviors that come from within, rather than being forced."[6]

Without preaching or insinuating a connection to any member of the audience, Jerry leans into his microphone and says, "My Sunday school teacher brought us a little Sunday school card. It had a picture of one of the prophets and Jesus on the front. And on the back was a story. She let us look at the picture and she read us the story. That's what caused this song to be wrote years later when I begin to think about how nice that was that they taught us about Jesus and let me know that there is a saving power, a saving grace, a power that was beyond my power. When I was powerless, Jesus would take over and guide my life for me. I want to sing you this song, it's called 'I Believe.'"[7]

As the song ends, Jerry steps to the microphone and introduces the next song. "This is an instrumental Marty and I wrote in memory of a friend of ours who used to play with us. He also played with Bill Monroe for many years. It's entitled 'Old Joe Stuart.'" Tammy smiles in recognition of Joe Stuart as the man who taught her fundamentals of singing, as her father kicks off the tune with a punchy guitar intro and Marty joins in on mandolin. With banjo, guitar, mandolin, and bass, and Jason Carter's soaring fiddle, the tune personifies bluegrass music at its ensemble best.

As he has throughout his career, Jerry continues to write songs that touch the inner reaches of the soul, songs based on personal experiences or those of others he has known. Grateful for the care given Tammy at the Place of Hope and hearing Coupe's story of recovery, Jerry wrote "Shadow of the Steeple." He premiers the song tonight.

"What caused me to write 'In the Shadow of the Steeple' was a service we had near Music Row in Marty Stuart's office. The first thing Mike Coupe told us was about himself. He did not make himself above you. He said, 'I used to live close to here. I lived right there, under the freeway.' And he began to tell how alcohol took over his life.

"He told us that you cannot take charge of these things, that God has to do it for you. It's Jesus. You've got to commit yourself to Him. This song is dedicated and done especially for Mike Coupe and the Place of Hope. I dedicate it to you folks. Listen, as Tammy sings."[8]

People are dyin' in the shadow of the steeple
Of the church standin' high on the hill
Down here in the city they have no pity
For the drunk lyin' cold and so still

I'm standin' on skid row, a place we all go
When the pressure of life breaks our will
Chained to our sorrow, no hope for tomorrow
And no one seems to care how we feel

CHORUS:
Wake up, O Zion, hear the cries of the dyin'
The harvest is ripe in the field
Light the candles of prayer for lost souls everywhere
And write it down: God's judgment is real

"Every one of us identifies with 'In the Shadow of the Steeple,'" says Rev. Coupe in an after-concert interview. "The fact that it was written out of a heart that can relate to people like us means everything. It says it all about what this life is like for us. Tammy just sings the fire out of it."[9]

While Jerry serves as emcee, introducing songs and sharing testimonies, Tammy prefers to minister through song. She is especially committed to songs that speak to and for women. Jerry and Marty wrote the meditative hymn, "At Calvary," for Tammy, who sings with the conviction of one who has experienced the sorrow and joy the song proclaims:

> A woman in pain that shows on her face
> Deep in her soul a war's taking place
> She's searching for peace, mercy and grace
> Woman, go with me, I know the place
>
> CHORUS:
> At Calvary, at Calvary
> Jesus is calling, come unto me
> At Calvary, At Calvary
> Bring me your burdens, I'm all that you need.
>
> A man with his fortune sits all alone
> In a mansion so fine, it's still not a home
> He longs for love, a companion to hold
> Rich man, go with me, find love for your soul
>
> CHORUS

"I think Tammy saw this might be a place she could come to and work out some things," says Coupe. "Tammy is in a unique position to really make an impact on young people, on women, and alcoholics and drug addicts. We sit in churches and don't think we have problems like this. The reality is, everybody knows somebody who needs help. There's such a problem in this world today that nobody's immune from it. Tammy can go into churches and tell them, 'This is where I come from. This is what happened to me.' And people respond to that truth."

The Sullivans end the concert as it began, with a vigorous version of "Morning Train." As the audience files out, Jerry and Tammy meet with fans, sign autographs, and bid goodnight to those who remain. Mike Coupe sits in the near-empty concert hall, reflecting on the program and feeling grateful for the Sullivans and their program. "We're just amazed at what we've been a part of tonight," he says. "The music was extraordinary. We're humbled by Jerry and Tammy that they would come here and do this for us and make us a part of this wonderful record. It not only documents who and what they are, but it will further their careers and more of America will get to know who they are as artists."[10]

The musicians load their instruments in their cars, say goodbye to Mike Coupe, and begin the 335-mile journey home.

Following a refreshing Wagarville break from touring, we're on the road again. This time, we're bound for Nashville and the Ryman Auditorium celebration, stopping briefly in Monroe, Louisiana, on the way.

In Monroe, we have lunch with Rev. Gerald Lewis, first cousin to Jimmy Swaggart, Mickey Gilley, and rock and roller Jerry Lee Lewis. Rev. Lewis is an athletic, trim 6'2" genteel Southern gentleman. He's attired in a white linen sport coat with Holy Ghost lapel pin, black slacks, a brown, black, and white tie with abstract print. His late-model Lincoln four-door sedan and gold rings on each hand with nickel-sized diamond settings attest to his financial success as twenty-eight-year pastor with the Assemblies of God church. Lunch is casual, and Brother Lewis does not shy from commenting on his cousins' excesses, apparently unaware of his own ostentations.[11]

After lunch, we meet Andy Griggs, a young man Stephanie met at a gospel sing. Andy and a friend will accompany us to Ryman Auditorium. Within two years, Andy and Stephanie will marry, Andy will sign a recording contract with RCA Records and will have a #2 hit with his debut single, "You Won't Ever Be Lonely."

We arrive in Nashville Monday, May 30, and park in the bus parking space behind the Ryman. Tammy carries Jerry's guitar as we approach the rear entrance. Jerry says to Tammy, 'I love you. I just want you to know that, bein' such a big help to daddy. I hate to lean on you so much, though." Tammy replies with words she's probably repeated hundreds of times, "That's okay. I don't mind."

Inside the auditorium, television crews set up their equipment while painters and carpenters hustle to finish their work converting the aged temple into a modern television studio set. An informal convention of country stars gathers on the stage, oblivious to the work going on around them. Grandpa Jones, Little Jimmy Dickens, Earl Scruggs, and Bill Monroe swap stories and renew friendships. From 1943 until 1974, the Ryman was home to the *Grand Ole Opry*, broadcast over Nashville radio station WSM. Here, the greats stood on stage and sang into its microphones. Hank Williams performed here. As did Kitty Wells, Patsy Cline, Marty Robbins, Dolly Parton, Faron Young, Loretta Lynn, and Bill Monroe. Elvis Presley performed here once. His rockabilly gyrations were not appreciated by the Ryman's conservative management, and Elvis was told not to return.

Oak display cases along the outer walls harbor artifacts from Opry stars, present and past: Hank Williams's gray suit and red silk tie; Kitty Wells's lavender dress with white and gold sequined hearts; Bill Monroe's iconic white Stetson hat; *Johnny Cash at Folsom Prison* gold record; glittering flowery Nudie suits of Hank Snow and Little Jimmy Dickens; and Marty Robbins's yellow racing suit.

Tuesday is scheduled for rehearsals. I accompany Jerry to the dressing room he shares with country luminaries, including Carl Perkins. Perkins's "Blue Suede Shoes," which he wrote and recorded in 1955 and Elvis recorded in 1956, stands as one of the iconic songs of early rock and roll. Perkins is neatly attired in a white western shirt with a fringe top. He wears a gold bracelet and rings sparkling with diamonds. Vince Gill, Leroy Parnell, Joe Diffie, and Hank Williams's fiddler Jerry Rivers and steel guitarist Don Helms gather around and entertain each other with stories of country and bluegrass characters they've known or worked with. Jerry and I are enthralled listening to adventures and misadventures in days of yore. Hal Ketchum stops in to speak with Jerry about their scheduled trio on Ferlin Husky's "Wings of a Dove."

This afternoon, we watch featured performers rehearse their songs to music provided by the house band of Nashville studio musicians. Jerry and his old boss and friend, Bill Monroe, stand together on stage catching up on family stories and careers. Around 4:00, rehearsals pause as the stage crew carries in a cloth covered booth with a lockbox time capsule inside. Country stars were asked to bring something personal to place in the time capsule which will be opened 50 years hence, in 2044. Jerry and I stand on stage and watch as Loretta Lynn, Vince Gill, Tammy Wynette and others tote their contributions into the booth and emerge empty-handed. I notice Jerry watching intensely, his expression a combination of incredulity and awe. "Jerry," I say, "they're going to open the time capsule in 2044." Staring straight ahead and with no change of expression, Jerry responds, "They think they are. If Jesus hasn't come back and got us all by then."[12]

Jerry is talking about the Second Coming of Christ, the day Christ calls together His souls, living and dead, and casts them upwards to Heaven, or banishes them to Hell. Jerry's comment brings into sharp focus the urgency with which he and Tammy minister with their songs and testimonies. For them, any hour of any day may be Judgment Day. And, aware of cultural trends they interpret as Satan-wrought decadence, they believe the end of the world is near, possibly in their lifetimes.

Wednesday, June 1, last minute rehearsals and film crew details consume most of the day. The concert will begin at 7:30 and by

Jerry Sullivan and Bill Monroe on stage, Ryman Auditorium, June 3, 1994. Photograph by Jack Bernhardt.

6:00, the stars are donning their stage outfits and getting ready for their turn in the spotlight. Marty Stuart sits patiently in the makeup chair, while his flowing black pompadour is trimmed and moussed. Loretta Lynn, Kitty Wells, and Patty Loveless, their hair in curlers, are rehearsing Kitty Wells's 1955 hit, "Making Believe." Lynn is having her green taffeta sequined dress pressed while wearing it.[13]

At 7:30, the stage lights are up and cameras roll as Kathy Mattea welcomes the audience at home and in the auditorium to the evening's celebration. Along with musical performances, archival footage and commentary from the stars provide context for the historic building, which is synonymous with the golden age of country music. The grand finale features the cast of stars joining the Sullivans on "Brand New Church" as the credits roll and the concert ends. On June 25, the show will be viewed by a nationwide audience on the CBS television network.

The next morning, we board the bus and begin the 370-mile journey to Wagarville. With tour and TV special behind them, Jerry and Tammy will prepare for their next adventure in church or festival or street fair or benefit concert, as they have done together for the past fifteen years.

Jerry Sullivan died May 31, 2014, the last of nine brothers and three sisters of his musically rich, faith-inspired family. April 20, 2017, Tammy succumbed to her battle with cancer. With their passing, along with the deaths of Enoch and Emmett Sullivan, the esteemed era of South Alabama bluegrass gospel music ministries drew to a close. Still, the legacy of Jerry and Tammy Sullivan and the Sullivan Family Gospel Singers endures with the ministry of Tammy's husband, Jonathan, and their son, Jon Gideon Causey. Their 2020 CD *The Greatest Story* showcases father and son on such Jerry Sullivan classics as "I Can See God's Moving Hand," "He Called My Name," and "I Want to Go to Heaven," along with the contemplative Jerry Sullivan/Marty Stuart hymn, "Pray."

Jerry Sullivan's songwriting partner and family friend, Marty Stuart, trusts the Sullivan legacy will remain strong as it moves forward in the capable hands of Jonathan and Jon Gideon. In his liner notes to *The Greatest Story*, Marty writes, "Jonathan has kept an eye on the manuscripts, notebooks, tapes and scraps of paper left in the wake of so many creative storms, and he keeps those songs alive by playing and singing them. I can't help but think how proud Tammy would be to hear Jon Gideon singing.

"He's got the family tones along with the cool factor to go with it. He is to be a standard bearer, no doubt, and a bona fide cat in the making."[14]

# Chapter 11

# Jonathan and Jon Gideon Causey
## The Gospel Road Goes on Forever

Thursday, April 13, 2023, is sunny and warm, a typical Louisiana spring afternoon. Jonathan Causey guides the bus along US 165 toward Lake Cove, Louisiana, where he and his son, Jon Gideon, will sing this evening at Happy Hollow Holiness Church. Since the COVID shut-down of 2020, bookings are hard to come by. Churches that were once reliable venues have shut their doors; others hold church service, but COVID worries remain and they are reluctant to host social events such as gospel concerts.

For the Causeys, this is especially troubling since their debut CD, *The Greatest Story*, was released in 2020 with no way to showcase the songs and sell product. But this weekend came together as a four-church tour, and Jonathan and Jon Gideon will perform one show each in Louisiana and Texas, and two in Mississippi. This part of Louisiana is familiar territory for Jonathan. He grew up in Lake Cove and lives today twenty miles away in Forest Hill with his wife, Callie Bates, and Jon Gideon. Jonathan steers the bus off the highway and makes a sharp turn onto Happy Hollow Road, a narrow dirt drive leading to the church.

Happy Hollow Holiness Church has changed little since I was here with Jerry and Tammy Sullivan in 1993. The fellowship hall has been removed, making the building, and plumbing has been installed. But the sanctuary is much as it was then. The most notable difference is David and Trisha Messer's seven children are now adults. Four are ministers, including daughter Cherry Messer Silva, thirty-one, who has succeeded her father as pastor.

Jon Gideon cuts a dapper figure in his pressed black trousers, vest, blue shirt, and tie. He sits confidently at the altar, playing his grandfather's storied guitar and singing Jerry and Marty's "Church Keep Moving On" with self-assurance, authority, and poise.[1] Jonathan stands on the opposite side, singing harmony and providing rhythmic backup with a guitar that once belonged to Ralph Stanley II, son of the late bluegrass icon, Ralph Stanley. Jonathan's brother, Daniel, had been playing bass on these church gigs. But Daniel has taken a job as a long-haul truck driver and is not available to join his brother and nephew on this tour. To compensate, Jonathan purchased a bass machine he can program to provide the rhythmic pulse for each song. Jonathan tells the audience he has "Dan in the Can," and they enjoy the joke.

During intermission, Brother David and Sister Trisha take the stage and reprise their "Devil's Level" performance of thirty years ago. This time, their daughter Cherry accompanies her parents on piano.

Some twenty-five listeners from Lake Cove and vicinity applaud Jon Gideon's performance of the songs Jerry and Tammy may have sung on each of the dozen or so occasions they performed here. Happy Hollow Holiness Church's founder and longtime pastor, Brother David Messer, has remained supportive of the Sullivans since they began their ministry in 1979. Grateful for Brother David's loyalty, Jerry and Tammy sang here often as a stop on tours that carried them through Louisiana into Mississippi, Texas, or Arkansas.

Six miles from Turkey Creek, Lake Cove is a small, unincorporated community nestled deep within the forests of Evangeline Parish. Lumbering is important to the economy, but carpenters and

Jonathan and Jon Gideon Causey performing at Happy Hollow Holiness Church, Lake Cove, Louisiana, April 13, 2023. Photograph by Jack Bernhardt.

roofers also find employment here. Jonathan's father established a roofing business and taught the trade to many of Lake Cove's young men, including his sons. Jonathan is one of twelve children born to J. A. and Genevie Causey. Two siblings died young, so his parents raised six boys and four girls. When Jonathan was a boy, there were no musicians in Lake Cove. But his oldest brother Mike and sister Marilyn formed a semi-professional gospel group, touring local churches. Sixteen years older than Jonathan, Mike taught his brother his first chords on guitar.

Jonathan's mother was the prayer warrior in the family. On Wednesday nights and Sundays, she made sure her children were dressed for church services at the United Pentecostal Church in Turkey Creek. Jonathan credits Genevie with guiding him toward his walk with faith. "My parents believed in the Pentecostal faith, just like Brother Jerry," he says. "My parents were raised up in the Pentecostal church in Turkey Creek. My mother was the faithful one in the family. If it wouldn't have been for her, probably none of us would have had the teaching that we had. She had us in church, come rain or shine. Every time the doors were open, we were in church."[2]

Inspired by his siblings' music, Jonathan dreamed of a gospel ministry of his own. The few opportunities to learn music in Lake Cove did not deter him from pursuing his passion. "I would hear people on recordings picking solos," he recalls. "I wanted to do that. So I prayed, 'Lord, if you will put me in front of people who would help me learn how to play this music, I will always do it for you.' I love all facets of music, but when it comes to performing professionally, I'm going to sing you a gospel song. That's part of my ministry and what God's called me to do."[3]

Jonathan's dreams began to materialize when Jerry and Tammy Sullivan performed at Brother David's church. Hearing of Jonathan's passion for learning music, Jerry invited Jonathan to stay with him in Wagarville during the summer between his junior and senior years of high school. "In 1984 I went to their home when I got out of school and stayed the summer," Jonathan recalls. "Brother Jerry promised my mother that I would be alright. That was the only way that she would let me go. I spent the summer then came back for my last year of school. The night after graduation in 1985, I left home and moved in with Brother Jerry. I stayed seven months."[4]

During his stays with the Sullivans, Jerry gave him pointers on playing guitar and, importantly, how to live successfully as a professional musician. "Jerry Sullivan was like a second dad to me. He taught me a lot about life, in general. Our daddy taught us a lot about work, but never so much about life and living on the road. Jerry Sullivan taught me so much about how to make it in the business and how to live and act on the road."[5] Throughout the 1980s, Jonathan traveled and performed with the Sullivans. In 1988, he contributed mandolin and vocals to the Jerry and Tammy Sullivan album *Authentic*. It was his first experience in a recording studio. "That was the first time I met Marty Stuart," Jonathan recalls. "He played guitar and mandolin on that record. He looked at me and asked, 'Is this your first recording?' I said, 'Yes, sir, it is.' He said, 'Are you having fun?' I was so nervous I didn't know if I was having fun," he says, laughing.[6]

Jonathan married in 1992. He and his wife gave birth to Savanah, who today lives with her daughter close to Forest Hill. The couple formed a gospel music duo, playing churches and tourist attractions, such as Six Flags Over Texas and the Ozark Folk Center in Mountain View, Arkansas. They recorded four albums, including *Aayeee! Louisiana*, featuring Cajun legend Jo-El Sonnier.

Following his divorce in 2000, Jonathan found work as a truck driver and roofer. He was trying to find his way back to the music when he received a phone call from his old friend, Tammy Sullivan.

"She encouraged me," he says. "She let me know that God had a purpose and that He had something for me to do. I was in Atlanta. She said, 'We're going to be in Birmingham. Why don't you come down and be with us? Just hang out with us.' After that, Tammy would invite me to play mandolin when I was off from work."[7] Tammy and Jonathan married in 2002. Jon Gideon was born on Saint Patrick's Day, 2004. Now, with decades of music ministry behind him, Jonathan follows Jerry's lead by teaching his son how to succeed as a gospel artist.

Jon Gideon was ten years old when his grandfather died. He was thirteen when his mother succumbed to her battle with cancer. But as an infant, Jon Gideon was already traveling the gospel highway to the backwoods churches that defined the Jerry and Tammy Sullivan ministry. One could say he was born, as his mother had said of herself, to tell the Gospel story.

With Jon Gideon's mother gone, parenting was the responsibility of his father, who chose to continue living in Wagarville. Like his mother and grandfather before him, Jon Gideon attended school in nearby Leroy. Midway through sixth grade, he left Leroy and,

Tammy Sullivan and Jon Gideon, on the road in Louisiana, 2005. Photograph by Jack Bernhardt.

with Jonathan's encouragement, began a distance learning program offered by Abeka Christian Academy of Pensacola, Florida. He graduated high school in 2022.

Along with schoolwork, Jon Gideon began guitar lessons with his father, who also helped his son understand the nuances of his mother's vocal style. Jon Gideon was born with spina bifida, a spinal disorder that affects walking and mobility. Believing his condition would impact Jon's ability to do physical labor, such as carpentry or roofing, Jonathan's music lessons were preparing Jon Gideon for a career in the music ministry.

"Jon was brought up in this music," Jonathan says. "He come up goin' on trips with us. By the time he was two, he'd been to four or five states across the South. I not only want to teach him about the music, but about life in general. It's giving him a foothold on life and Christianity, and learning to perform on his own. Jon is very Christian-oriented. He loves his church. We go to Elwood Baptist Church in Forest Hill right now. He feels he has a calling in this ministry. He wants to do this."[8]

Early Friday morning, Jonathan steers the bus westward, on the 185-mile journey to Onalaska, Texas. Jonathan is a long-haul veteran, adept at handling the 1998 forty-five-foot-long Prevost bus as he was transporting produce and poultry from California on eighteen-wheel behemoths. By noon, we pull into the parking lot of Wildwood Gospel Church, where the singing will take place this evening. For Jerry and Tammy, Wildwood was a special church community, and remains so for Jonathan and Jon Gideon. A gospel sing at Wildwood was like coming home, and one might say the Causeys will be singing to the choir.

Wildwood Church was founded by a deejay from Houston in 1971 in the region of Polk County known as Hodge Bottom. The area was originally settled as a land grant, with the stipulation that residents were required to be members of the Hodge clan. With echoes of old-timey brush arbors, services were initially held outdoors beneath a live oak tree.

"Not far from where the church is located now is Open Bottom Creek," says Wildwood pastor Dennis Hodge. "Everybody who lived back there was Hodges at the time. We all lived on the hill. When I was a child, it was called Hodge Hill. Later the county called it Hodge Bottom. The church that was started was not far from that creek bottom. It was under a big live oak tree. When I was a kid, there would be ten to fifteen of us kids, and we'd crawl up on the big tree limbs and sit and listen."

Within a few years, a small church was built in Hodge Bottom. At times, the church was cramped, accommodating perhaps fifty people. Dennis Hodge recalls, "If the Sullivans came, they would have to open the back doors and folks would stand on the porch and listen. The old church was about a mile back in the woods. The bridge wasn't very good and people would end up in the creek. Or they'd call my grandad and ask him to come down with his loggin' truck and pull them to the church."[9]

The Hodges continued to worship in the Hodge Bottom Church until 1989. Elders Debra and Shorty Hodge envisioned purchasing land and building a new church beside Farm-to-Market Road 356 (FM 356). Their vision became reality in 1989. Recently renovated, the church has grown its rolls to some 125 members, equally divided between Hodge and non-Hodge families.

The Sullivans regarded Wildwood Church as family since Tammy's first husband, the late JR Johnson, grew up and attended church here. "I met Tammy for the first time when she married my childhood friend JR," says Debra Fletcher Hodge who, along with her husband Elton "Shorty" Hodge is a former pastor and current elder of Wildwood Church. "That was in the early eighties. JR's dad had pastored my childhood church. JR and I spent quite a bit of time together. My husband and I were pastoring a church at the time so we invited Jerry and Tammy down. JR was playing piano for the group, and Jerry and Tammy came to our church for the first time in 1982."[10]

The Sullivans were revered by the Wildwood Church community for the authenticity of their music and sincerity of their mission. They often stopped by to visit the Hodges' home while en route to other venues. "The first image I get is sitting around our table and chatting," recalls Sister Debra. "And them telling stories of growing up with music.

"We loved their music because it was bluegrass and we were raised country. It was part of our heritage. The audiences loved it because they were so open. It was an anointing that you felt the spirit of God move when they began to sing. Their songs were songs that you related to, things that were going on in real life.

"You knew they were Biblically based. It didn't bother them for you stand or to shout 'Amen,' or to clap. You were encouraged to be a part of what they were doing. They let us know they were human, that they had emotions. Their music conveyed to you that they had been there, that they knew what you were doing in everyday life and going through, and that they were there to minister to you. When Tammy stepped on that stage, she was your best friend singing straight to you. I always felt it was a privilege to know someone who had that type ministry."[11]

Tonight, it's Jonathan and Jon Gideon who sing for the congregation of Wildwood Church. The audience numbers forty-eight, including six children. The set list consists of Sullivan standards, along with a few selected songs and tunes to highlight the vocal and instrumental talents of Jon Gideon. From the prolific catalog of Sullivan songs, the performers have culled Sullivan Family favorites, along with ones written by Jerry and Marty Stuart.

Jon sings lead on "Claim the Victory," an up-tempo promise of salvation from their *The Greatest Story* CD, the born-again anthem "He Called My Name," and the Margie Sullivan standard "Old Brush Arbors." He showcases his versatility as a flat-picking guitarist with a medley of fiddle tunes: "Soldier's Joy," "St. Anne's Reel," and "Whiskey Before Breakfast," which Jon has renamed "Jesus Before Breakfast" because, he says, "Nobody wants whiskey in church."[12]

In his testimony, Jonathan reminds the church of the Sullivans' brush arbor origins, and that one of Sister Margie's most popular songs is relevant today. "We probably have very few here that remember the brush arbor days," he says. "There was no electrical instruments at that time. But they had the rhythms that they put together and was able to fashion a style of music that resonated with people. The mainest thing is that they come up with songs that had messages.

"Jon is gonna do a song that comes from that era," he says. "Sister Margie recorded this many years ago, but it still has

Jonathan and Jon Gideon Causey perform at Wildwood Gospel Church, Onalaska, Texas, March 2023. Photograph by Jack Bernhardt.

meaning today. What I mean is, it's just around the corner that we're gonna have a change, Brother Dennis. God is gonna tolerate the world as it is for just so long. It states in the Bible that in the last days, people will call good evil, and evil good. That's the times we're in. I want you to listen to the message as Jon sings, because it's about 'The Change.'"

> I'm tellin' you there'll be a change after awhile
> Where we now wear a frown there'll be a smile
> We may suffer pain and loss and Jesus died upon the cross
> That we might have that change after awhile.[13]

The Causeys honor a request by pastor Dennis Hodge, who asks for "At the Feet of God," the Grammy-nominated song that was one of Tammy's most requested. And, reflecting upon Jon's performance of "Tomorrow," Debra Hodge says, "Jon is an extension of his mother. He poured his heart into the words and the music and into the performance. It was so Tammy. She gave everything she had every time she stepped on the stage. That's what I saw in Jon Gideon. If you closed your eyes, it was like hearing the old Sullivans, Brother

Jerry and Sister Tammy. That says to me, no, this music is not lost. It's being carried on through Jon Gideon."[14]

It's no mystery that Jon Gideon resembles his mother's singing in tone and style. Genetics plays a role. But so does Jon's familiarity with the music of his mother and grandfather. As Jonathan remarked, Jon traveled with the family from the time he was in diapers. He heard their songs before he could talk.

When he decided to follow in their footsteps, he listened to their recordings and studied the mechanics of singing of both Jerry and Tammy.

"I would go with them about every trip," Jon Gideon recalls. "Sitting in the audience, I would listen to them. At home, they would practice. So hearing them over and over, listening to the songs and how they sung and played them, sort of ingrained it into me. It was somewhat difficult to learn to play an instrument I'd never played. And to sing in ways I'd never sung. But taking inspiration from such a good singer as my mama, it showed me a path. She showed me a path to follow with all the albums they had. I listened to those a lot.

"When I first started singin', I wasn't able to hear very well the finer details of the songs. But over the past five years, I've become more in tune with some of the turns, the accents that my mom put into her songs. She would change the notes in such a way that it had a different feel than to just sing it plainly. She put a feelin' in it. She put a lot of emotion into her songs and you could hear that. I try to emulate that. I try to put my feeling into each of the words I sing."[15]

When Tammy was learning to sing by following the path blazed by cousin Margie, her father counseled her to also listen to other vocalists, and find her own voice. Jonathan offers similar advice to Jon Gideon. "Dad said while it's good to listen to Mama and learn how she sung, he wanted me to listen to other people. How they sing certain songs and how they express themselves. He wanted me to listen to other singers and see what I liked and what I didn't, and take bits and pieces.

"I have my own playlist that I listen to—Ricky Skaggs, Nashville Bluegrass Band. I have a playlist on Spotify with several Nashville Bluegrass Band albums. Also, some Larry Sparks, Doyle Lawson, IIIrd Tyme Out.

"Another part of my singin' is that I took some inspiration not only from Mom but also from my grandfather. Specifically, the song 'Walking Through the Fire.' I try to emulate some of how he sings that. I try to incorporate a bit of both Mom and my grandfather."

In addition to songwriting and singing, Jerry Sullivan was renowned for his guitar playing. With his father's guidance, Jon is working on patterning his playing after grandfather's. "I've been trying to dabble in that kind of style. For instance, 'I Can See God's Moving Hand.' Daddy taught me that break based on what my grandfather did. But I also go on the internet and watch different people who do fiddle tunes."[16]

The concert ends on a high note, with the Causeys' stirring rendition of "Church Keep Moving On." The pews empty, and audience and performers retreat to the fellowship hall where a welcomed dinner of fried chicken and desserts awaits. Afterward, Jonathan eases the bus onto the highway and we begin the 390-mile trip to Raleigh, Mississippi.

En route to Raleigh, the three of us discuss musicians, songwriters, and songs. Jon Gideon entertains himself scrolling through his cell phone. While this is a new route for us, the landscape seems familiar. We pass a Full Gospel Church with a model oil derrick standing tall beside its message board. Farther on, we see the Bear Arms shooting ranges and His and Hers Mercantile, a welcome relief from the ubiquitous Dollar General and Dollar Tree stores we pass along the way.

In Raleigh, Jonathan and Jon Gideon sing an 11:00 a.m. concert at High Hill Baptist Church and a 6:00 p.m. session at Liberty Baptist Church. Each concert reiterates, in playlist and performance, those from Happy Hollow and Wildwood. Thirty adults and six children attend the High Hill Baptist performance, while eighty-three adults and seventeen children gather at the larger Liberty Baptist Church, both in Smith County, Mississippi.

With the bus loaded and diesel in the tank, we begin the 235-mile journey home to Forest Hill. For Jonathan and Jon Gideon, this was a successful tour. Jon Gideon gained another weekend of valuable experience, singing and playing the family songs. With each outing, he seems more committed to a life of a touring gospel artist, singing and playing the kinds of church communities served by the Sullivans for seventy-five years.

"Papa told me the Sullivans would never forget the small churches because that's where they started," Jon Gideon says. "That's where I started, too. I want to play for those little churches, but I also want to play for the bigger crowds at festivals. I want to try to gain as much following as they had, to gather as much influence and be able to convey the message, to tell the Gospel.

"I want to continue to sing these songs my mother and grandfather, and the Sullivan Family did. I want to keep singin' them for the people, and tell them about the Lord. I want to do this for as long as my life on Earth will let me."[17]

# Chapter 12

# Reflections on Fieldwork and Discovery
## *The Changer and the Changed*

In 1978 I left New York City on my thumb, hitchhiking to the Appalachian Mountains for two weeks of solitary backpacking and calm. Emerging from several days in the back country, I came upon a small stream not represented on the US Geological Survey topographic map I was using to find my way back to the Skyline Drive. My immediate reaction was confusion: "This stream is not supposed to be here," I told myself. Then, in a jolt, I realized the stream was, indeed, "supposed" to be there: the stream was natural, the map cultural. Society's reliance upon our cultural topographic maps often distorts our perception of reality and misleads us into mistaking cultural representations for natural truths. Through this incident, a fleeting moment in my backpacking retreat, I learned to look carefully for dissonance or congruence, and not to rely exclusively on "received wisdom," which is ever-changing and often misconstrued as inerrant.

I carried this lesson with me into my adventures with the Sullivans. I resolved to guard against allowing preconceptions to influence my work with an evangelical subculture of which I had no direct experience. Raised in the North and graduate schooled in New York City, I am aware that many Americans retain an image of the South as it was during Civil Rights strife of the 1960s, or as portrayed in the 1972 film *Deliverance*. Much of this imaging is an invention of the cultural cartographers of Hollywood and New York, many of whom may have never stepped foot south of the Mason-Dixon Line.

The Sullivans' ministry is important for the exceptional quality of their work and role-model devotion. It is important, too, because generationally Jerry and Tammy straddled the transition between the old and new South, between the South of Jim Crow and the South of civil rights. The South I experienced with the Sullivans and Causeys is one in which family and faith are central to individual goals and social life. Kin networks and faith communities are for many the source of emotional and spiritual support, as well as material assistance when times are spare. The nexus of family is for many the church, which historically has been and continues to be among the most important social institutions in the South.

My travels with Jerry and Tammy Sullivan took me to venues with eclectic audiences—folk festivals, college classrooms, Ryman Auditorium, and the Place of Hope, among them. But most performances I witnessed took place in churches, either as part of the service or scheduled concert. Musically ecumenical, the Sullivans performed in Baptist and United Methodist churches, and even the Church of Ireland, yet most singings took place in holiness or Assemblies of God and especially, Jesus Name Pentecostal churches in the Deep South. I heard sermons, testimonies, and prayers for personal salvation, physical healing, and divine intervention for a successful outcome of an impending event. I heard pastors and guest preachers speak out against what they consider sins of cultural decay, and call for restoring civility and responsibility to social life.

The ministry of Jerry and Tammy, and carried on by Jonathan and Jon Gideon Causey, is based upon a brilliant body of songs composed by Jerry, and by Jerry and Marty Stuart. They are songs that celebrate life yet look forward to life after death in the arms of God. Their testimonies and songs are interwoven and combine personal experiences with those of the listener. The Sullivans and their audiences share the same concerns, fears, and challenges that trouble many Americans, regardless of how they are expressed in the ballot box.

Wherever Jerry and Tammy performed, one theme consistently emerged. When asked to characterize the Sullivans' ministry, pastors and members of their congregations, musicians and fans used the words "real," "authentic," "anointed." At a time when religion had fallen into disfavor due to scandals within the Catholic church and the excesses of celebrity televangelists, the Sullivans retained the trust of their audience. It was a trust based upon decades of performing and presenting themselves as one with, rather than apart from, their audience. The Sullivans were committed to their ministry. They were willing to shoulder hardship and sacrifice in order to share their songs of inspiration, believing their reward awaited in the Kingdom of God.

I am neither more nor less agnostic than when my association with the Sullivans began in 1993. As an anthropologist, I view religion through an anthropological lens. Religion is universal. All societies, including those diverse as the Yanomami of Amazonia, the Dani of highland New Guinea, the Azande of Africa's Sudan, and the Sullivans of Washington County, share belief in the supernatural and a form of life after death. The Sullivans and Causeys respect my views as I respect theirs. We never attempted to convert each other to our respective systems of belief. This allowed me freedom to pursue my questions, and Jerry and Tammy, Jonathan and Jon Gideon were free to answer them without fear of being judged.

When the ethnographer steps into a community for study, it begins a process of reciprocal change in which both ethnographer and the community studied are transformed. An enduring change with the Sullivans was our friendship. Jerry and I enjoyed each other's company, and regarded each other as friends. We took each other places we likely would never have been, saw and heard things we would not have experienced. Jerry and Tammy carried me with them to churches and their communities and, by introducing me in concert and sanctioning my work, made sure I was welcomed. This made my work easier and more complete. Through them, I came to know the strength and conviction, doubts and fears of a faith community I had not previously understood.

I brought Jerry and Tammy to North Carolina and facilitated concerts and classroom discussions at Elon University, University of North Carolina, and North Carolina State University. I wrote promotional material for Jerry and Tammy, and was honored when asked to write liner notes for their *Tomorrow* and *Live at the Place of Hope* CDs. I donated field tapes, interviews, and photographs to the Southern Folklife Collection at UNC-Chapel Hill. I think that visiting the SFC and seeing his work on display was one of Jerry's proudest moments, knowing his legacy will be available to students and scholars for generations to come.

My goal writing this book has been to provide a case study documenting the musical ministry of Jerry and Tammy Sullivan and through them to illuminate the lives of individuals, families, and communities served by the Sullivans and other gospel ministries in the Deep South. Brother Arthur and family began their professional career in 1949 on radio, and evangelized backwoods churches with testimony and song. Thirty years later, Jerry and Tammy began their father-daughter ministry. They served some of the same communities that had welcomed Enoch and Margie, while establishing their own fans until Jerry's death in June 2014. Professional tensions at times enflamed familial passions. Yet, I believe each branch of Sullivan gospel complemented the other, while bringing inspiration to their supporters, old and young.

To borrow a term from the Millennial generation, the Sullivans were "old school" in their approach to faith. Regions of the South remain strong in adherence to Bible-based Christian values. Yet, as Lighthouse Chapel of Tioga pastor C. Pat Carrington laments, attracting young worshippers can be a redoubtable challenge. As Jon Gideon grows in his ministry, he may win favor with younger audiences that remain elusive in "old school" churches with "old school" demands.

As this chapter was being written, Margie Sullivan, the "First Lady of Bluegrass Gospel," passed away at age ninety. With her passing, the celebrated era of Sullivan gospel in Washington County has sung its final collective chord. Still, the music and legacy live on as the center shifts from Alabama to Louisiana. As Jonathan and Jon Gideon go forward with their ministry, they may continue to serve loyal supporters, such as the Happy Hollow Holiness and Wildwood Gospel communities. They may also win new fans in larger churches, urban and suburban, and discover, as Brother Jerry did, that "the road is very much alive" to Jon Gideon's fourth generation gospel ministry. It's a mission that in Jon Gideon's words, will allow him to show his fans "how I feel about the Lord, and hopefully bring them closer to Him through the songs."[1]

# Afterword

## The Brush Arbor Trail

One of the great heroes of faith you will meet here in the pages of Jack Bernhardt's *Bluegrass Gospel: The Music Ministry of Jerry and Tammy Sullivan* is Reverend Glenn Sullivan. "Brother Glenn," as he is known to his friends and loved ones, is the pastor and overseer of the Victory Grove Church in Wagarville, Alabama. Victory Grove was founded in 1949 by Glenn's father, the Reverend Arthur Sullivan, and serves as the home church, genesis, and legacy ground of the Sullivan Family and all of its gospel-singing heirs. Tradition runs deep in the church and within its pastor. A beautifully written passage from Mr. Bernhardt describes the Bible from which Brother Glenn preaches: "Brother Glenn's King James Bible, written in older style English language, gives scripture a sort of verbal patina, bestowing upon it the authority and wisdom of antiquity." The same can be said of the songs, stories, sermons, testimonies, prayers, and declarations of faith that echo in the walls of Victory Grove Church.

There are generations of like-minded pilgrims who have been part of a primarily southern backroads circuit of music-loving churches (like Victory Grove), which Jerry Sullivan coined "the Brush Arbor Trail." In the early twentieth century, sectors of rural southerners gathered to worship in structures built of small timbers with rafters covered in brush. They were known as brush arbors. Over time, many of these humble outdoor sanctuaries evolved into the country churches that define the Brush Arbor Trail. The trail's collective congregation has a high concentration of kindhearted people with insightful views of the natural, as well as the supernatural, worlds—honorable souls who often exude a Christlike otherness, neighborly people whose songs, customs, and sacred rights were handed down from the old-world order of family and beyond. The churches along the Brush Arbor Trail are beloved touchstones bound by covenant to the sanctity of Heaven. They are as iconic in the hearts of their communities as the great cathedrals have been to centuries of faithful Europeans.

The name Sullivan is highly regarded all along the Brush Arbor Trail. Beginning in the early 1950s, the Sullivans brought their music out of the backwoods of Alabama. They pioneered the circuit of playing music at churches, camp meeting revivals, political rallies, fairs, car dealerships, auditoriums, and festivals in towns throughout the southern states. Running late more often than not, with dust billowing out from behind their car, the Sullivan family pulled up to the job with tires screeching. Former Sullivan bandmember Bob Burnham said, "Enoch doesn't arrive. He comes in for a landing." The family was usually met by friends and helpers who grabbed instruments, the sound system, the record box, and clothes bags in order to get the show going. The Sullivan men were a sight to behold, rolling out in their jet-black suits, white shirts, colorful ties, and patent leather shoes. They were larger-than-life, exotic, handsome gentlemen with rustic movie star appeal. Enoch, Emmett, and Jerry had wild hair. Enoch and Emmett sported razor-thin William Powell-styled mustaches that only enhanced their outsider mystique. Sister Margie was an all-business soldier of the cross whose traditional Pentecostal look added authenticity and an unadorned beauty to the troupe. When everything was finally in place, Enoch had a classic opening line that went something like, "Yes sir, the Sullivan Family and Sister Marge, we're here and ready to go. We weren't running late, brother; we were just a little behind. But none of God's good people are gonna get left behind on that day." Then the music started. When they began playing "Traveling the Highway Home," all was forgotten, and time disappeared.

Beginning with radio broadcasts hosted by Reverend Arthur Sullivan in the late 1940s, Enoch, Emmett, Margie, Jerry, and, later, Tammy Sullivan were all airwave personalities. The Sullivan Family went on to make records and host their own television show, which ran for numerous seasons and was widely syndicated throughout the South. From the first of their traveling days, the Sullivans' celebrity drew scores of people to witness the family's unorthodox and exciting concept of combining the gospel story with their high-powered, fiddle- and banjo-driven string band sound, all the while presenting it as church music. In truth, the Sullivans led the charge and did for their side of the river what Jerry Lee Lewis did for his in regard to paving the way for freedom of musical expression in conservative, white houses of worship. The earth is bound to have "shook" when the Sullivans stepped up to the pulpit and plowed into a thinly veiled version of Ervin T. Rouse's fiddle tune, the "Orange Blossom Special," while passing it off as the "Gospel Train." At the end of the number, I'd like to imagine a dreamlike frost of rosin drifting down from Enoch Sullivan's fiddle bow onto the floor, forever sealing the presence of the fiddle in God's house. Later in the same decade, at a seminary in Waxahachie, Texas, the walls came down when Jerry Lee Lewis was expelled for making a boogie-woogie piece out of Kenneth Morris's sacred masterpiece "My God Is Real." It cannot be denied that such musical breakthroughs (while pretty much already in place at most Black churches) were instrumental in making inroads and building bridges between the church and the burgeoning country, rhythm and blues, and rock and roll industries.

The Sullivan Family no doubt looked to Bill Monroe, the Stanley Brothers, Flatt and Scruggs, Wilma Lee and Stoney Cooper, Roy Acuff, the Chuck Wagon Gang, the Carter Family, the Bailes Brothers, Hank Williams, and the like for inspiration. However,

they had only the Lord and themselves to look to when it came
to surviving and marching their brand of rhythm-based music
through the churchyards. Beyond the sound and feel of the music,
what further set the Sullivan Family apart in a special way was the
quality of songs that Jerry Sullivan wrote for the group. His songs
were of the same caliber as fellow Alabamian Hank Williams. Both
men's compositions take up very little room on a piece of paper but
their words, while simple, are vast, powerful, heart-filling, and life-
changing. I was twelve years old when my dad, John Stuart, and a
neighbor named John Wesley Cook, and I traveled from our hometown of Philadelphia, Mississippi, one Saturday to the National
Guard Armory building in Jackson, Alabama, to watch the famous
Sullivan Family and the Father of Bluegrass, Bill Monroe, put on
a full gospel concert. It was a hot, holiness gathering with lots of
applause and shouting. Two songs that evening absolutely stole the
show. Bill Monroe repeatedly encored his 1950s classic "I've Found
a Hiding Place" and when Enoch Sullivan finally called "Uncle"
Jerry Sullivan forth from behind the bass and turned him loose at
the front-and-center position, he tore the place completely apart
with his "I'd Rather Be on the Inside Looking Out (Than to Be on
the Outside Looking In)." It received four encores. Monroe would
score five later in the evening. I never had the privilege of witnessing Elvis Presley (who was a child of the Mississippi Brush Arbor
Trail) perform in his prime, but I've seen enough footage of his early
performances to know that Elvis and Jerry used the same brand
of dynamite on an audience when their moment in the spotlight
rolled around.

The Jackson, Alabama, concert was an intense and thrilling happening that ignited something inside of me. I traveled home that
night with a mandolin pick in my pocket that Bill Monroe had given
me (along with instructions to "Take that home and learn how to
use it"), autographed albums by the Sullivan Family as well as Bill
Monroe, and a heart full of encouraging words that Jerry Sullivan
had offered me regarding being a musician.

A few months passed, and word went around my neighborhood that the Sullivan Family was coming to town to play at a church one mile from our house. My Louisville, Mississippi, pal Carl Jackson, had recently joined the Sullivans to play some shows. I called Carl and persuaded him to ask Enoch Sullivan if I could bring my mandolin and play a song. Enoch welcomed me, the song was well received, and I proclaimed the night a big victory. Later that year, when school was dismissed for the summer, I again persuaded Carl to ask Enoch if I could go on the road with the Sullivans. For reasons known only to God and the angels, Enoch said yes. My parents consented. A few days later, Carl came and picked me up in his yellow Ford Gran Torino, and we traveled from Mississippi to Alabama to join the Sullivans.

I found myself the latest in a long line of dreamers who stepped up to travel the Brush Arbor Trail. From the middle position in the backseat of Brother Enoch's Town & Country station wagon, sitting between Carl Jackson and "Link" Dickerson, I witnessed the mystery of an unknown future unfold, the sun of my spirit rising. It was a touching yet melancholy poem, and I loved every word of it. I welcomed every mile of the journey along with all the scenes along the way: vegetable gardens; roses, gladiolas, and irises; the scent of magnolia on the breeze; country churches; decaying towns with abandoned movie theaters; rusty water tanks with the town's name trying hard not to fade away; cheap motels; burger barns, chicken shacks, and catfish cabins; mighty oaks next to slumbering pines that cast long shadows; a million miles of kudzu vines; crows looking down from highline poles; American flags, Confederate flags, and Christian flags; performing at George Wallace rallies; playing on the recording of a "live" album; cut-rate service stations with pictures of George Wallace on the wall and Mountain Dews in a cooler filled with dingy water; Moon Pies, Tom's peanuts, and Nabs; cemeteries; negotiating atmospheres of unrest; traveling over innocent land with a dark, moody undercurrent left behind by the Civil War; spotting lost traces of old America; girls; applause; signing autographs; trying to discern the sheep from the wolves; country cooking; staying at church folks' houses; truck stops with gravel parking lots; ponds; nice people with names like Aunt Susie, Aunt Elva, Uncle Homa Lee, Brother Dub, Sister Bonnie, and Brother Abe Areno; the man Emmett called "Brother Positive Post" because he was always happy; the glamorous lady Emmett referred to as "Miss America" who followed the Sullivans; Emmett's never-ending repertoire of loveable nonsense and pranks; seeing a chain-smoking monkey at a Stuckey's the same day as witnessing a man handle a serpent at a church; hearing someone speak in tongues for the first time; using Sunday school rooms as a place to tune our instruments and change clothes; rotary-dial phone calls home to my folks; talking nonstop about music and staying up late without consequences; having a late-night wreck in Brother Enoch's car; listening to the Grand Ole Opry pop and crackle on Brother Enoch's car radio as we rode through the southern darkness, telling myself that someday I'd get to play there; the smell of the earth, the smell of cheap perfume, and the smell of drugstore cologne; lots of beehive hairdos; the synchronicity of the passing of the trains alongside of the rhythm of the music that we were playing. Those are the things I remember when I close my eyes and think back on the summer of 1972. I saw nothing but pure beauty in it all. The cares of the world, the sins of the past, didn't exist during that season. There were no locked doors in my pathway. Love and encouragement, acceptance, handshakes of affirmation, and beautiful prayers prayed over me were the hallmarks of my journey. It remains one of the happiest times of my life.

Those three months on the road were a rite of passage, the downbeat of an epic with eternal overtones. The quality of the experience with the Sullivan Family is immeasurable. At the end of the summer, Carl Jackson took me home. The ninth grade was calling. I felt as though the circus had set me out on the edge of town and then rolled on out of sight. That didn't work for me. I had seen another side of life and came to believe I was a part of it. I was a pitiful excuse for a student. Less than a month into the school year, I was expelled.

One week later, I was on stage at the Grand Ole Opry, playing along-side Lester Flatt. I've seldom slowed down since—I went on to see the world with Lester's band, then Johnny Cash's band, and finally, my own band. A sour record deal, a divorce, and my reckless and rowdy ways brought the glory days that began on the Brush Arbor Trail to a halt in 1987. In the midst of the bleakest of those times, Jerry Sullivan called to ask, "Do you know of a mandolin player that might be available to work some upcoming concerts that me and Tammy have booked?" I told him that I did, "Me." A week later, I found myself back on the Brush Arbor Trail, tuning up in the same Sunday school rooms from nearly two decades earlier. The images on the walls that reminded me "Jesus loves you" were still present. The scenes and the people along the Trail were still poetical, regal in manner, but on this tour, they suggested a somber benediction of days gone by. As I attempted to put my life back together, I was met with a fresh round of love, acceptance, understanding, and compassion. I quickly realized that the people along the Brush Arbor Trail were well versed in welcoming prodigals back home after they'd burned out in the material world and needed a helping hand to get back to where they once belonged, as the famous song says. I loved playing music with Jerry and Tammy. It was pure joy. My routine became driving back and forth from Nashville, usually for a weekend run of concerts. Jerry, Tammy, sister Stephanie, Jonathan Causey, and me. That was the cast. We rode the highways and byways in Jerry's early 1960s Silver Eagle bus that he later named the Gospel Plow after one of the songs we wrote. Jerry and Tammy's ministry was a hip-pocket operation, held together by spit, glue, duct tape, guitar capos, love, prayer, and divine favor. I stood in amazement so many times when there seemed to be no way out: blown tires, transmission failure, headlights that wouldn't work, no heat, no pay after a church service which meant no fuel for the bus or food for the band. The list goes on, but Jerry Sullivan never wavered in his faith or belief that "the Lord will reach down and take care of the matter." And, the Lord always did. I witnessed it time and time again.

I remember thinking more than once, "This is not a life for the faint of heart." No cross, no crown.

The Lord also reached around and poured the gift of songwriting onto Jerry and me. Our first collaboration involved putting words to a Bill Monroe instrumental called "Get Up John." After that, the floodgates opened. Lyrics and melodies seemed to be waiting on us everywhere we went. We wrote songs going down the road in the Gospel Plow, in the Jug Jungle, at Zelma Sullivan's kitchen table, by the Gulf of Mexico, in cafes, in the backrooms of churches, at people's homes we were visiting, under trees, and in Jerry and Zelma's garden next to the tomato vines. On one of my early trips to Wagarville to play a New Year's Eve service at Victory Grove Church, Jerry and I wrote more than twenty songs over the course of the weekend. We actually worried about running out of paper. Every one of those songs was a solid keeper that Jerry and Tammy went on to record.

Tammy Sullivan was a powerhouse of a proclaimer, a natural-born gospel singer with a timeless voice. Mahalia Jackson, Sister Rosetta Tharpe, and Martha Carson would have no doubt considered her one of their contemporaries. It was an honor to write for her. It was also an honor to write with Jerry. The songs we created together are anointed, seemingly touched by the flame of the divine fire. Jonathan Causey, along with his and Tammy's son Jon Gideon, are the keepers of those sacred documents now. I rest in knowing that those songs are in the best of hands with two of the last Sullivan-related proclaimers on the Brush Arbor Trail. The Causey boys offer the songs a future. Stephanie Sullivan also witnessed many of those songs come into existence. They are a part of her; she is an heir to their legacy. My hope is that those songs will touch others with the same amount of comfort, encouragement, hope, love, and compassion they still bring to me. When I left the Brush Arbor Trail at the end of summer 1972, I took its gifts with me. On my second pass, while attempting to put myself back together before returning to the bright lights at the end of 1988, I again took the trail's gifts with me out into the world, namely Jerry and Tammy. This time, however, I left behind my part of those cherished songs that Jerry and I wrote as an offering of gratitude to the people of the Brush Arbor Trail. Those songs are indeed for everyone, but their power and the warmth of their words are at their fullest in those churches and in the hearts of the people along that mysterious old southern trail that's largely unknown to the rest of the world.

In 1993 Jack Bernhardt set foot on the Brush Arbor Trail for the first time. A respected anthropologist armed with ethics, guidelines, and hard-earned knowledge handed down from the claustral realm of academia, this student of rational process and aesthetic clarity shook hands with the mystical worlds of Brush Arbor religion, bluegrass gospel, and music ministry of the Deep South. It was an assignment of awesome proportions that he completed in 2023. Jerry and Tammy Sullivan, as well as their music, are now documented for the ages with integrity and honor. This book is a pure reflection of lives spent in divine service. Mr. Bernhardt describes Jerry Sullivan's face as "a complex interplay between kindness and pain." In a broader sense, that quote is an honest assessment of the entire story told within these pages. Jack Bernhardt nobly placed himself inside the story. Only his heart can tell how much of the story became a part of him.

*Marty Stuart*
Congress of Country Music
Philadelphia, Mississippi

# Notes

## Prologue

1. Clifford Geertz, "Waddling In," *New York Times Literary Supplement* (June 7, 1985), 623–24.

## Chapter 1. Getting Acquainted

1. Field notes, April 15, 1993.
2. Zelma Sullivan interview, May 26, 1994.
3. Jerry Sullivan interview, April 15, 1993.
4. Field notes, April 15, 1993.
5. Elva Sullivan Powell interview, May 26, 1994.
6. Elva Sullivan Powell interview.

## Chapter 2. The Sullivans of Washington County

1. Jacqueline Anderson Matte, Doris Brown, and Barbara Wadell, *Old St. Stephens: Historical Records Survey*, rev. ed. (St. Stephens, AL: St. Stephens Historic Commission, 1999).
2. Uncredited writer, "Alabama's Lost Capital," *Elements: On the Road to Old St. Stephens* (McIntosh, AL: Ciba Specialty Chemicals, 1999).
3. Field notes.
4. Robert P. Stockton, ed., *The History of Washington County: First County in Alabama*, Vol. 2 (Chatom, AL: Washington County Historical Society, 1989).
5. Thomas Lawson Jr., *Logging Railroads of Alabama* (Birmingham: Cabbage Stack Publishing, 1996), V.

6. Jerry Sullivan interview, April 17, 1993.

7. Jerry and Tammy Sullivan, cassette recording, *The Old Home Place* (NMS-1002, 1981).

8. Enoch and Margie Sullivan with Robert Gentry, *The Sullivan Family: Fifty Years in Bluegrass Gospel Music* (Many, LA: Sweet Dreams Publishing, 1999).

9. Jerry Sullivan interview.

10. Jerry and Tammy Sullivan, CD recording, *A Joyful Noise* (CMF-0160, 1991).

11. Jerry Sullivan interview.

12. David Reed, "Aspects of the Origins of Oneness Pentecostalism," in Vincent Synan, ed., *Aspects of Pentecostal-Charismatic Origins* (Plainfield, NJ: Logos International, 1975).

13. H. Richard Niebuhr, "The Doctrine of the Trinity and Unity of the Church," *Theology Today* 3 (1946), 371–84.

14. Elaine J. Lawless, *God's Peculiar People: Women's Voices and Folk Tradition in a Pentecostal Church* (Lexington: University Press of Kentucky, 1988).

15. Jerry Sullivan interview.

16. Thomas Goldsmith, *Earl Scruggs and Foggy Mountain Breakdown: The Making of an American Classic* (Urbana: University of Illinois Press, 2019).

17. Jerry Sullivan interview.

18. Enoch and Margie Sullivan with Robert Gentry, *The Sullivan Family*.

19. Enoch and Margie Sullivan interview, Saxapahaw, NC, April 16, 2005.

20. Jerry Sullivan interview with Marty Stuart, Jerry and Tammy Sullivan, *Tomorrow* (Ceil CD-2005, 2000).

21. Enoch and Margie Sullivan interview.

22. Enoch and Margie Sullivan with Robert Gentry, *The Sullivan Family*.

23. Jerry and Tammy Sullivan, *Time and Eternity*, Cassette JTS 100490 (1990).

## *Chapter 3. Serve the Lord with Gladness: Make a Joyful Noise*

1. This study centers on gospel music in predominantly White churches and communities in the American South. For discussion of gospel music in the African American community, see Jerma A. Jackson, *Singing in My Soul: Black Gospel Music in a Secular Age* (Chapel Hill: University of North Carolina Press, 2004); and Glenn Hinson, "Gospel Music, African American," *The New Encyclopedia of Southern Culture*, Vol. 14, Glenn Hinson and William Ferris, eds., "Folklife," 110–15 (Chapel Hill: University of North Carolina Press, 2009).

A version of this chapter was published in *The New Encyclopedia of Southern Culture*, Vol. 14, Glenn Hinson and William Ferris, eds., "Folklife," 115–21 (Chapel Hill: University of North Carolina Press, 2009).

2. Jack Bernhardt (2009).

3. Lois Blackwell, *The Wings of a Dove: The Story of Gospel Music in America* (Brookfield, MO: Donning, 1978).

4. Victor Turner, *The Ritual Process* (New York: Aldine de Gruyter, 1969).

5. Jack Bernhardt, "Performance, Faith, and Bluegrass Gospel: An Anthropological Journey with Jerry and Tammy Sullivan," in Charles K. Wolfe and James E. Akenson, eds., *Country Music Annual 2001*, 51–69 (Lexington: University Press of Kentucky, 2001).

6. Neil V. Rosenberg, *Bluegrass: A History* (Urbana and Chicago: University of Illinois Press, 1985).

7. Howard Dorgan, *The Airwaves of Zion: Radio and Religion in Appalachia* (Knoxville: University of Tennessee Press, 1993).

8. *Silent Witness: A Tribute to Country Music's Gospel Legacy*, Vol. 1 (Sony 66974 CK, 1994).

9. Field notes.

## Chapter 4. Love, Loss, and the High Lonesome Sound

1. Jerry Sullivan, author interview, July 14, 1993.

2. Jerry Sullivan, author interview.

3. Jerry Sullivan, author interview.

4. Bill Monroe, author interview, October 24, 1988.

5. Bill C. Malone, *Country Music U.S.A.* (Austin: University of Texas Press 1965). 10SIL

6. Rosenberg, *Bluegrass: A History*, 231.

7. Bill Monroe, cited in Thomas Goldsmith, liner notes to Bill Monroe and His Blue Grass Boys, *Crying Holy unto the Lord* (MCA Records MCAC 10017, 1991).

8. Bill Monroe, cited in Alice (Gerrard) Foster and Ralph Rinzler, liner notes to Bill Monroe and His Blue Grass Boys, *A Voice from on High* (Decca Records DL 75135, 1969).

9. Fred Bartenstein and Curtis W. Ellison, eds., *Industrial Strength Bluegrass: Southwestern Ohio's Musical Legacy* (Urbana: University of Illinois Press, 2021).

10. Jerry Sullivan interview.

11. Dean Mathis, personal communication.

12. Jerry Sullivan interview.

## Chapter 5. A Strength by Me: Jerry, Tammy, and New Beginnings

1. Jerry Sullivan, author interview, May 30, 1994.

2. Uncredited writer, "Group's Suits Seek $1 Million in Damages," *Clarion-Ledger*, Jackson, Mississippi. May 14, 1977.

3. Tammy Sullivan, author interview, April 17, 1993.

4. Jerry Sullivan, author interview, May 30, 1993.

5. Jerry Sullivan interview.

6. *Country Voice Records Present Jerry and Tammy Sullivan*, (cassette, NMS-1001, 1979).

7. Field notes, April 23, 1993.

8. "Mississippi River Flood of 1927," Britannica.com, https://www.britannica.com/event/Mississippi-River-flood-of-1927

9. Jerry Sullivan, author interview, April 23, 1993.

10. David Messer, author interview, January 19, 2005.

11. Field notes, April 24, 1993.

12. Field notes.

13. Field notes.

14. Wilbur Ansley, author interview, April 25, 1993.

15. Wilbur Ansley, author interview.

16. Jerry Sullivan, field notes, April 25, 1993.

## Chapter 6: Tammy Sullivan: Praise the Lord for This Life I'm Living

1. Tammy Sullivan, author interview, June 1, 2005.

2. Tammy Sullivan, author interview, April 17, 1993.

3. *Country Voice Record Present Jerry and Tammy Sullivan.*

4. Tammy Sullivan interview.

5. Tammy Sullivan interview.

6. Jack Bernhardt, "Cry Holy unto the Lord: Tradition and Diversity in Bluegrass Gospel Music," in *In the Spirit: Alabama's Sacred Music Traditions*, Henry Willett, ed. (Montgomery, AL: Black Belt Press, 1995), 108.

7. Tammy Sullivan interview.

8. Field notes.

9. Tammy Sullivan, author interview, June 3, 2005.

10. Tammy Sullivan interview.

11. Tammy Sullivan, telephone interview, August 27, 2000.

12. Tammy Sullivan, author interview, June 2, 2005.

13. Report of Investigation, Washington County Court Case CC 2003 000168.00. November 19, 2003.

14. Jonathan Causey, telephone interview, August 5, 2020.

# Chapter 7: Traveling the Gospel Highway from Potholes to Praise

1. Field notes.
2. Jack Bernhardt, "Gospel Music, Brush-Arbor Style," *News and Observer* (Raleigh, NC), April 7, 2003, 1C.
3. Marty Stuart, author interview, January 16, 2005.
4. Marty Stuart interview.
5. Marty Stuart interview.
6. Field notes.
7. C. Pat Carrington Interview, Ball, Louisiana, May 27, 2005.
8. C. Pat Carrington interview.
9. C. Pat Carrington interview.
10. Field notes.
11. Wayne C. Howell interview, Colfax, Louisiana, May 28, 2005.
12. Field recording, May 28, 2005.
13. Field recording.
14. Field recording.
15. Wayne C. Howell interview.
16. Field notes.
17. Field recording by the author, May 29, 2005.
18. Field notes, May 30, 2005.

# Chapter 8. Brother Arthur and Brother Glenn: From Brush Arbor to Victory Grove

1. Glenn Sullivan, author interview, May 29, 1999.
2. Enoch Sullivan, author interview, April 16, 2005.
3. Dixon D. Bruce Jr., *And They All Sang Hallelujah: Plain-Folk Camp Meeting Religion 1800–1845* (Knoxville: University of Tennessee Press), 1974.
4. Neil V. Rosenberg, *Bluegrass: A History* (Urbana: University of Illinois Press), 1985.
5. William Lynwood Montell, *Singing the Glory Down: Amateur Gospel Music in South Central Kentucky, 1900–1990* (Lexington: University Press of Kentucky, 1991).
6. Jack Bernhardt, "Cry Holy unto the Lord," 101–10.
7. Lois S. Blackwell, *The Wings of a Dove*; Don Cusic, *The Sound of Light: A History of Gospel and Christian Music* (New York: Hal Leonard, 2002).
8. Elaine J. Lawless, *God's Peculiar People: Women's Voices and Folk Tradition in a Pentecostal Church* (Lexington: University Press of Kentucky, 1988), 5.
9. Glenn Sullivan interview, Wagarville, Alabama, June 4, 2005.

10. Patricia D. Beaver, *Rural Community in the Appalachian South* (Lexington: University Press of Kentucky, 1986), 58.

11. Glenn Sullivan, author interview, May 29, 1999.

12. Field recording, January 19, 2005.

13. Field recording, January 19, 2005.

14. Robert P. Stockton, *The History of Washington County: First County in Alabama*, vol. 2 (Chatom, AL: Washington County Historical Society, 1989).

15. Field notes, April 20, 1993.

16. Field recording by the author, Victory Grove Church, December 15, 1999.

17. Sheriff William J. Wheat, author interview, May 27, 1994.

18. Glenn Sullivan, author interview, June 4, 2005.

19. Uncredited author, *Washington County News*, Chatom, Alabama, June 1, 2005.

20. Michael V. Angrosino, *The Culture of the Sacred: Exploring the Anthropology of Religion* (Long Grove, IL: Waveland Press), 145–53.

21. Glenn Sullivan, author interview, May 29, 1999.

22. A copy of the song folio is in the collection of the author.

23. Tape recording, Brother Arthur and family broadcasting on WJDB, Thomasville, Alabama, 1957.

24. Glenn Sullivan, author interview.

25. Jerry Sullivan, author interview, May 29, 1999.

26. Field recording, April 21, 1993.

27. Field recording by the author, April 16, 1993.

## Chapter 9. Trials, Troubles, Tribulations, and Heavenly Rewards

1. Field notes, May 28, 1994.

2. Field recording, May 28, 1994.

3. Tammy and Stephanie Sullivan, author interview, April 21, 1993.

4. Lorraine Lawless, *God's Peculiar People*, 36.

5. Werner Enninger, "Clothing," in *Folklore, Cultural Performances, and Popular Entertainments*, Richard Bauman, ed., 217–24 (New York: Oxford University Press, 1992).

6. Elva Sullivan Powell interview, Wagarville, Alabama, May 30, 1999.

7. Robert M. Anderson, *Vision of the Disinherited: The Making of American Pentecostalism* (New York: Oxford University Press, 1979).

8. Center for Population Studies, Census of Population and Housing (Oxford: University of Mississippi, 1990). https://sdc.olemiss.edu/1990-census-data/

9. *Pentecostal Praises: A Complete Church Hymnal (Shape Notes Only)* (Hazelwood, MO: Pentecostal Publishing House), 1947.

10. *Banner Hymns (Shaped Notes Only)* (Cleveland, TN: White Wing Publishing House), 1957.

11. Field Recording, April 21, 1993.

## Chapter 10. *From Lester Flatt to the Place of Hope and the Mother Church*

1. Marty Stuart with Jack Bernhardt, "In the Footsteps of a Good Man: Coming of Age with Lester Flatt," *Bluegrass Unlimited*, December 1992, 24–32.

2. Field Notes, Otto, Arkansas.

3. Place of Hope Brochure.

4. Mike Coupe interview, Place of Hope, January 8, 2007.

5. Field recording, January 8, 2007.

6. "Empathy," *Psychology Today*. www.psychologytoday.com/us/basics/empathy.

7. Jerry and Tammy Sullivan, *Live at the Place of Hope* (San Rydge Music SRDG 5001), 2007.

8. Field Recording, January 8, 2007.

9. Mike Coupe interview.

10. Mike Coupe interview.

11. Field notes, Monroe, Louisiana.

12. Field notes, June 1, 1994.

13. Field notes, June 1, 1994.

14. Marty Stuart, liner notes, Jonathan and Jon Gideon Causey, *The Greatest Story*, Uncle Jug Music (no number), 2020.

## Chapter 11. *Jonathan and Jon Gideon Causey: The Gospel Road Goes on Forever*

1. Field recording, Happy Hollow Holiness Church, Lake Cove, Louisiana, April 13, 2023.

2. Jonathan Causey interview, April 16, 2023.

3. Jonathan Causey interview.

4. Jonathan Causey interview, August 5, 2020.

5. Jonathan Causey interview, June 4, 2005.

6. Jonathan Causey interview.

7. Jonathan Causey interview.

8. Jonathan Causey interview, April 16, 2023.

9. Dennis Hodge interview, Onalaska, Texas, April 14, 2023.

10. Debra Hodge telephone interview, March 20, 2023.

11. Debra Hodge telephone interview.
12. Jon Gideon Causey interview, April 14, 2023.
13. Field recording, Wildwood Gospel Church, Onalaska, Texas, April 14, 2023.
14. Debra Hodge telephone interview.
15. Jon Gideon Causey interview.
16. Jon Gideon Causey interview.
17. Jon Gideon Causey interview, Forest Hill, Louisiana, April 23, 2023.

## Chapter 12. *Reflections of Fieldwork and Discovery: The Changer and the Changed*

1. Jon Gideon Causey interview, Forest Hill, Louisiana, April 24, 2023.

# Bibliography

Anderson, Robert M. *Vision of the Disinherited: The Making of American Pentecostalism.* New York: Oxford University Press, 1979.

Angrosino, Michael V. *The Culture of the Sacred: Exploring the Anthropology of the Sacred.* Long Grove, IL: Waveland Press, 2004.

*Banner Hymns (Shaped Notes Only).* Cleveland, TN: White Wing Publishing House, 1957.

Bartenstein, Fred, and Curtis W. Ellison, eds. *Industrial Strength Bluegrass: Southwestern Ohio's Musical Legacy.* Urbana: University of Illinois Press, 2021.

Beaver, Patricia D. *Rural Community in the Appalachian South.* Lexington: University Press of Kentucky, 1986.

Bernhardt, Jack. "Gospel, White." In *The New Encyclopedia of Southern Culture,* Vol. 14, Folklife, edited by Glenn Hinson and William Ferris, 115–21. Chapel Hill: University of North Carolina Press, 2009.

Bernhardt, Jack. "Gospel Music, Brush Arbor Style." *News and Observer,* Raleigh, NC, April 7, 2003, 1C.

Bernhardt, Jack. "Performance, Faith, and Bluegrass Gospel: An Anthropological Journey with Jerry and Tammy Sullivan." In *Country Music Annual 2001,* edited by Charles K. Wolfe and James E. Akenson, 51–69. Lexington: University Press of Kentucky, 2001.

Bernhardt, Jack. "Cry Holy unto the Lord: Tradition and Diversity in Bluegrass Gospel Music." In *In the Spirit: Alabama's Sacred Music Traditions,* edited by Henry Willett, 101–25. Montgomery: Black Belt Press, 1995.

Blackwell, Lois S. *The Wings of a Dove: The Story of Gospel Music in America.* Brookfield, MO: Donning Publishers, 1978.

Boles, John B. "Evangelical Protestantism in the Old South: From Religious Dissent to Cultural Dominance." In *Religion in the South,* edited by Charles Reagan Wilson, 13–34. Jackson: University Press of Mississippi, 1985.

Center for Population Studies. Census of Population and Housing. Oxford: University of Mississippi Press. 1990. https://sdc.olemiss.edu/1990-census-data/.

Cusic, Don. *The Sound of Light: A History of Gospel and Christian Music.* New York: Hal Leonard, 2002.

Dixon, Bruce D., Jr. *And They All Sang Hallelujah: Plain-Folk Camp Meeting Religion 1800–1845.* Knoxville: University of Tennessee Press, 1974.

Encyclopedia Britannica. "Mississippi River Flood of 1927," 1974. https://www.britannica.com/event/Mississippi-River-flood-of-1927.

Enniger, Werner. "Clothing." In *Folklore, Cultural Performances, and Popular Entertainments,* edited by Richard Bauman, 217–24. New York: Oxford University Press, 1992.

Foster, Alice (Gerrard), and Ralph Rinzler. Liner notes to Bill Monroe and His Blue Grass Boys, *A Voice from on High.* Decca Records DL 75135, 1969.

Geertz, Clifford. "Waddling In." *Times Literary Supplement,* June 7, 1985, 623–24.

Goldsmith, Thomas. *Earl Scruggs and Foggy Mountain Breakdown: The Making of an American Classic.* Urbana: University of Illinois Press, 2019.

Goldsmith, Thomas. Liner notes to Bill Monroe and His Blue Grass Boys, *Crying Holy unto the Lord.* MCA Records MCAC 10017, 1991.

Lawless, Elaine J. *God's Peculiar People: Women's Voices and Folk Tradition in a Pentecostal Church.* Lexington: University Press of Kentucky, 1988.

Lawson, Thomas, Jr. *Logging Railroads of Alabama.* Birmingham: Cabbage Stack Publishing, 1996.

Malone, Bill C. *Country Music U.S.A.* Austin: University of Texas Press, 1965.

Matte, Jacqueline Anderson, Dorris Brown, and Barbara Wadell. *Old St. Stephens: Historical Records Survey,* rev. ed. St. Stephens, AL: St. Stephens Historic Commission, 1999.

Montell, William Lynwood. *Singing the Glory Down: Amateur Gospel Music in South Central Kentucky, 1900–1990.* Lexington: University Press of Kentucky, 1991.

Niebuhr, H. Richard. "The Doctrine of the Trinity and Unity of the Church." *Theology Today* 3 (1946): 371–84.

*Pentecostal Praises: A Complete Church Hymnal (Shape Notes Only).* Hazelwood, MO: Pentecostal Publishing House, 1947.

Psychology Today. "Empathy." www.psychologytoday.com/us/basics/empathy, no date.

Rosenberg, Neil V. *Bluegrass: A History.* Urbana: University of Illinois Press, 1985.

Stockton, Robert P., ed. *The History of Washington County: First County in Alabama,* vol. 2. Chatom: Washington County Historical Society, 1989.

Stuart, Marty (with Jack Bernhardt). "In the Footsteps of a Good Man: Coming of Age with Lester Flatt." *Bluegrass Unlimited* 27, December 1992.

Sullivan, Enoch, and Margie Sullivan (with Robert Gentry). *The Sullivan Family: Fifty Sullivan Years in Bluegrass Gospel Music.* Many, LA: Sweet Dreams Publishing, 1999.

Uncredited author. "Crime Reports." *Washington County News*, Chatom, AL, June 1, 2005.

Uncredited writer. Report of Investigation, Washington County Court Case CC 2003 000168.00. Washington County, AL, November 19, 2003.

Uncredited writer. "Alabama's Lost Capitol." *Elements: On the Road to Old St. Stephens*. McIntosh, AL: Ciba Specialty Chemicals, 1999.

Uncredited writer. "Group's Suits Seek $1 Million in Damages." *Clarion-Ledger*, Jackson, Mississippi, May 14, 1977.

# Recommended Listening

## Compact Discs

*A Joyful Noise*, CMF 016D, 1991.
*At the Feet of God*, New Haven Records CD07569, 1995.
*Tomorrow*, Ceili Records, 2000.
*Live at the Place of Hope*, San Rydge Music, SRDG 5001, 2007.
Uncle Jug Sullivan, *The Great Revival Meeting*, no label, no date.
Jonathan and Jon Gideon Causey, *The Greatest Story*, Uncle Jug Music (no number), 2020.

## Audio Cassettes

*Country Voice Records Present Jerry and Tammy Sullivan*, NMS-1001, 1978.
*The Old Home Place*, NMS-1002, 1979.
The Sullivans, *Come on Down*, San Rydge Records (no number), 1987.
The Sullivans Jerry, Tammy, and Jr, *Authentic*, San Rydge Records (no number), 1988.
*Time and Eternity*, JTS 100490, no date.
*How Great Thou Art*, banjo instrumental featuring Emmett Sullivan, JTS-001, no date.

# Index

# About the Author

**Jack Edward Bernhardt** is a well-traveled anthropologist who holds an MA from Kent State and MPhil from Columbia University. His fifty-year career includes archaeology, folklore, ethnography, and journalism. From 1987 through 2020, he served as country and traditional music correspondent for Raleigh, North Carolina's *The News and Observer*. His work has appeared in *The New Encyclopedia of Southern Culture*, *The Bluegrass Reader*, *In the Spirit: Alabama's Sacred Music Traditions*, *North Carolina Folklore Journal*, *The Encyclopedia of Country Music*, *Bluegrass Unlimited Magazine*, *Caves and Culture*, and other publications. Jack has also lectured widely on Southern music, from the North Carolina Center for the Advancement of Teaching to the Appalachian and Bluegrass Music Festival in Omagh, Northern Ireland, and has taught courses on archaeology and the culture of country music at Elon University and the University of North Carolina at Chapel Hill. He lives in Hillsborough, NC, with his wife, Lisa, their Yellow Labrador, and two cats.